PENGUIN MODERN MASTERS
KARL MARX

David McLellan was born in England in 1940 and educated at Oxford, the University of Paris, and the University of Frankfort. He is presently a Reader in Political Theory at the University of Kent, and he has lectured in the United States at Princeton, Northwestern, Vanderbilt, and other universities. His previous books include *The Young Hegelians and Karl Marx, Marx before Marxism,* and *Karl Marx: His Life and Thought.*

Frank Kermode, King Edward VII Professor of English Literature at Cambridge, is the author of *The Classic; D.H. Lawrence; Shakespeare, Spenser, Donne;* and other widely acclaimed critical studies.

MODERN MASTERS

PENGUIN
MODERN MASTERS

EDITED BY frank kermode

*By Modern Masters we mean the men who
have changed and are changing the life and
thought of our age. The authors of these volumes are themselves masters, and they have
written their books in the belief that general
discussion of their subjects will henceforth be
more informed and more exciting than ever
before.* —F.K.

CONTENTS

BIOGRAPHICAL NOTE

1818	May 5, birth of Marx.
1835	Study at University of Bonn.
1836	Study at University of Berlin.
1837	Letter to his father.
1838	Death of father.
1841	Submits doctoral thesis.
1842	Articles for *Rheinische Zeitung*.
1843	Marries Jenny von Westphalen; moves to Paris; critique of Hegel's *Philosophy of Right*; "On the Jewish Question."
1844	Editor of *Deutsch-französische Jahrbücher; Economic and Philosophical Manuscripts*.
1845	Moves to Belgium; *Theses on Feuerbach*.
1846	*The German Ideology*.
1847	Joins Communist League.
1848	*The Communist Manifesto*. Moves to Germany to edit *Neue Rheinische Zeitung*.
1849	*Wage-Labor and Capital*. Moves to London.
1850	*The Class Struggles in France*.
1852–62	Articles for *New York Daily Tribune. The Eighteenth Brumaire of Louis Bonaparte*.

1857–58 *The Grundrisse.*
1859   *Critique of Political Economy.*
1862–63 *Theories of Surplus Value.*
1863   Death of mother.
1864   Foundation of First International; Inaugural
        Address.
1865   *Value, Price and Profit;* composition of *Capital,*
        Volume Three.
1867   *Capital,* Volume One.
1869   Engels moves to London.
1871   The Paris Commune; *The Civil War in France.*
1875   *Critique of the Gotha Programme.*
1881   Death of Jenny Marx.
1882   Preface to second Russian edition of *The Communist
        Manifesto.*
1883   March 14, death of Marx.

The inaccuracies in the obituary of Karl Marx published in the London *Times* are an indication of how little he was known when he died. But in the century or so since his death, Marx's name—whether revered or reviled—has become known to all. Paradoxically, this widespread influence has not always aided the comprehension of what Marx had to say. In the sphere of politics this is understandable: as part of the ideological equipment of mass movements, Marx's writings have too often been reduced to ill-digested slogans. And their piecemeal publication has meant that only recently has a coherent picture been able to emerge. So it is not surprising that Marx still remains so misunderstood. It is simply not true, for example, that Marx ever described the historical process as a movement of thesis, antithesis, and synthesis; or that his ideas were refuted by the Russian

Revolution in that, according to him, a revolution had to come about in the most advanced industrial countries; or that he believed the standard of living of the working class would inevitably decline; or even—on a more personal level—that he lived in enforced poverty and died at his desk. Yet all these statements are widely believed.

These misapprehensions are all the more striking when the extent of Marx's influence is considered: no more than seventy years after his death one third of the world lives under political systems claiming direct inspiration from Marx's ideas, and his followers are a force to be reckoned with everywhere else in the other two thirds. Intellectually, Marx's influence has been as great as it has been politically, and this influence is not only confined to the obvious subjects of politics, economics, and history. There is scarcely a discipline to which scholars working from a "Marxist" point of view have not brought insights. To take two rather surprising examples: in the field of literary criticism, the work of the Marxist George Lukács is gaining increasing attention; and one of the most influential schools of theology on the Continent stems from Ernst Bloch's interpretations of the young Marx. It is not only in sociology that development can largely be described as a dialogue with the ghost of Marx.

There are several reasons why Marx himself is so elusive. Marx was a thinker on the grand scale. In a world of increasing specialization, it becomes difficult to follow a thinker who not only mastered so many disciplines but also managed to integrate them. This broadness of his sweep was due to several factors: Marx was a cosmopolitan, rootless, Jewish émigré intellectual; he had moved rapidly from the idealist hyperintellectual opposition movements in semifeudal Germany, through the perfervid socialist sects of Paris, to mid-Victorian England ("the demiurge of the bourgeois universe" as he called it); he received a classical education and was steeped in a philosophy that drew its inspiration from antiquity in general and the aristocratic ideal of the Greek *polis* in particular. When tired of economics, Marx relaxed by reading Thucydides and the classical authors that were "ever new." He read all Aeschylus in the original every year. He was one of the last renaissance men.

This cultural breadth inherited from Germany matched well with the general enthusiasm for system-building and all-embracing theories of the Victorians. Marx was in a good position to observe Victorian capitalism: in 1851, two years after he arrived in London, the Great Exhibition opened in which, as he put it, "the world bourgeoisie erects its pantheon in the new Rome where it proudly places on show the deities it has fabricated." And 1867, the year in which Marx published Volume One of *Capital*, marked the height of the liberal era. It was an age of manifold inventions, of swiftly increasing supplies of all sorts of goods and services, an era in which progress could be, and was, charted almost daily. There was also a greatly enlarged range of facts at the disposal of the researcher, and a "realism" made itself felt everywhere from the politics of Bismarck to the novels of Zola. Above all, science was making spectacular advances and Comte had already given a name to the final and supposedly all-embracing science—sociology. This sense of progress and realism was fully absorbed by Marx along with the confidence in the values of freedom, democracy, and rationality that were common to all thinkers in that period of exceptional middle-class stability.

But to say that Marx was a Victorian is not to deny that he has anything to say to our more stormy times. Marx's method of analysis has survived even where its content is no longer of great interest. The broad question with which Marx tried to come to grips—the causes and destiny of the economic revolutions of his time—is with us still. Above all, the delicate dialectic between progress and catastrophe haunts the present generation as much as it did Marx: "At the same pace that mankind masters nature, man seems to become enslaved to other men or to his own infamy. Even the pure light of science seems unable to shine but on the dark background of ignorance. And our invention and progress seem to result in endowing material forces with intellectual life, and in stultifying human life into a material force."

KARL MARX

The Life

i

EARLY YEARS

When Marx wrote in *The Communist Manifesto*
that as the class struggle approaches its decisive hour a section of enlightened bourgeois
intellectuals would join the proletarian cause, he
may well have had himself in mind. For he was
born, in 1818, into a comfortable middle-class
home in Trier, the commercial capital of the
Moselle winegrowing district, the oldest city in
Germany, and one of the most beautiful. Two
factors predisposed him to take a critical look at
German society. First, he came from a long line
of rabbis on both sides of his family: his father,
although intellectually a typical rationalist of the
Enlightenment who knew his Voltaire and Lessing by heart, had only agreed to baptism as a

Protestant on pain of losing his job as one of the most respected lawyers in Trier; his mother, whose horizons were bounded by the problems of her household, was strongly influenced by Jewish piety. Second, there was strong opposition in the Rhineland to its domination by semifeudal Prussia. For the Rhineland not only was the most advanced area of Germany industrially but had been annexed by Napoleon and much influenced by the principles of the French Revolution.

Having spent five rather undistinguished years in Trier High School, Marx went to the University of Bonn in 1835 at the age of seventeen. There he enrolled in the Faculty of Law, was strongly receptive to the romanticism dominant at Bonn, and spent a lot of time drinking, dueling, and writing poetry dedicated to Jenny von Westphalen, to whom he had become engaged the same year. Jenny was the daughter of Baron von Westphalen, a city counselor in Trier who had already interested Marx in romantic literature and Saint-Simonian politics before his departure for Bonn.

Marx's father considered that his eldest son was not living up to his high expectations at Bonn and sent him to the far larger and more serious-minded University of Berlin in 1836. Here Marx remained for the next four years. He wrote innumerable poems, a complex classification of legal concepts three hundred pages long, a comic novel, a tragic play, and a new basic system of metaphysics. With the astonishing capacity for rapid assimilation that distinguished him all his life, he filled notebook after notebook, moving from law toward philosophy, and finally abandoning romanticism

in favor of the Hegelianism then dominant in Berlin—
an intellectual evolution that Marx described in a long
and fascinating letter to his father. He summarized his
newly acquired view: "if the gods had before dwelt
above the earth, they had now become its center." Very
soon, Marx abandoned his formal studies and began to
prepare a doctoral thesis. He was spending a lot of his
time in the company of the radical Young Hegelian intellectuals, led by Bruno Bauer, who were engaged in
turning the destructive side of Hegel's dialectic against
his system and moving from a critique of religion to one
of politics. Marx's thesis had the rather obscure subject
of the difference between the atomic theories of Demo-
critus and Epicurus, but like most of the Young Hegelians he saw a parallel between post-Aristotelian and
post-Hegelian philosophy.

The thesis completed, Marx had hoped to obtain a
position teaching in a university through the good
agencies of Bauer, but Bauer himself was dismissed for
unorthodoxy in early 1842. More or less disowned by his
mother (his father had died in 1838), Marx decided to
try to make a career out of journalism. His reputation
as a mordant critic was high among his Young Hegelian friends, one of whom described him as follows:
"He combines the deepest philosophical seriousness with
the most biting wit. Imagine Rousseau, Voltaire, Hol-
bach, Lessing, Heine, and Hegel fused into one person—
I say fused, not juxtaposed—and you have Dr. Marx."

In the spring of 1842, Marx began writing for the
Rheinische Zeitung, an opposition daily backed by liberal
Rhenish industrialists. He contributed articles on the

freedom of the press and on religion in politics, and, in October, he became editor. The paper's circulation increased by leaps and bounds, but increasing difficulties with the censorship authorities led to its suppression in March 1843.

Marx was not unhappy to be freed from his editorship: he was, as he put it, "head over heels in love" and made immediate preparations for his marriage to Jenny —they had been engaged for seven years. Instrumental in the suppression of the *Rheinische Zeitung* had been Marx's exposé of the miserable poverty suffered by the Moselle winegrowers, a piece of work that led him, as Engels said later, "from pure politics to economic relationships and so to socialism." But, first of all, Marx felt the need to return to his studies and to come to terms with Hegel's political philosophy. This he did in the summer of 1843, staying at his mother-in-law's house in Kreuznach. He read Rousseau, Montesquieu, and Machiavelli, as well as numerous historical works on the French Revolution. In the resulting unpublished manuscript, entitled "Critique of Hegel's Philosophy of Right," Marx definitively rejected Hegel's idealistic justification of contemporary German politics.

PARIS AND BRUSSELS

Marx decided to emigrate to Paris. For several months he had been discussing with one of his Young Hegelian friends, Arnold Ruge, the possibility of producing a Franco-German journal to unite German theorizing with the progressive politics of the French; and Paris, the hothouse of innumerable socialist sects, made an ideal center. Marx arrived there in October 1843 and settled in the Latin Quarter, sharing a house—as an experiment in community living—with his coeditor and other German exiles. Marx's contributions to the *Deutsch-Französische Jahrbücher* were two articles "On the Jewish Question" and an "Introduction" to the manuscript on Hegel's political philosophy that he hoped to publish later. But contact with workers' clubs and the general political atmosphere of Paris made a rapid impression on Marx, and his growing communist tendencies led to a break with Ruge. The *Deutsch-Französische Jahrbücher* failed to attract French collaboration or make itself commercially viable and never got beyond its first issue. But Marx continued his reading on the French Revolution and began to turn his attention to the classical English economists. Ruge found the pace altogether too fast: "Marx reads an enormous amount; he works with uncommon intensity and has a critical talent that sometimes degenerates into a wanton dialectic, but he finishes nothing, is always breaking off and plunging afresh into an endless sea of books."

As summer 1844 wore on, Marx conceived the plan of writing a series of monographs dealing with law, morals, politics, and so on, and began to collect material for the first one on political economy. These notes became known as the "Economic and Philosophical Manuscripts" or "Paris Manuscripts" and contained extracts from the English economists, a description of humanistic communism as an alternative to contemporary alienated society, and a critique of Hegelian philosophy.

Marx passed a lot of time with the poets Heine and Herwegh, fellow exiles, and the Russian anarchist Bakunin, and spent whole nights discussing the Hegelian dialectic with Proudhon, the leading French socialist.

In September a lifelong friendship and collaboration was born when Friedrich Engels met Marx in Paris. Engels was the son of a Rhenish cotton spinner whose firm had a branch in Manchester, where Engels had been working. He brought Marx a practical acquaintance with the workings of capitalism, an ever-ready source of financial assistance, and the one firm friendship that Marx enjoyed throughout his life. Engels stayed two weeks in Paris, almost all the time talking to Marx. The two friends decided to collaborate on a book attacking Bauer and their former Young Hegelian colleagues. The polemic, ironically entitled *The Holy Family*, was scarcely finished when Marx was expelled from Paris for subversive journalism.

Marx settled for the next three years in Brussels, where there was a considerable German émigré population and a comparatively free press. Before leaving Paris he had signed a contract for a book on economics and politics, and in the summer of 1845 he began to renew his studies of economics with a visit to England where Engels acted as guide. During the last three months of 1845 the two friends were engaged in writing *The German Ideology*, which set out their newly acquired materialist conception of history and was designed to "settle accounts with our erstwhile philosophical consciousness."

While in London, Marx had met the leaders of the

League of the Just, a semiclandestine organization of émigré German artisans whose headquarters had originally been Paris. In Brussels Marx founded a network of communist correspondence committees to keep German, French, and English socialists informed about each other's ideas and activities, and to try to introduce a minimum of theoretical unity into the nascent communist movement. In this context, two important disputes occurred during 1846. In the first, Marx opposed in the Brussels Committee the views of Weitling, a journeyman tailor who advocated an imminent revolutionary insurrection. Marx's view was that "the bourgeoisie must first come to the helm," and he prevailed. Secondly, Marx wrote the *Poverty of Philosophy* to oppose the eclectic socialism of Proudhon, whom he had previously invited to represent Paris on the network. This is how Marx appeared to Annenkov, a Russian émigré, who met him just as he was beginning to make an appearance in the German working-class movement:

Marx himself was the type of man who is made up of energy, will, and unshakable conviction. He was most remarkable in his appearance. He had a shock of deep black hair and hairy hands and his coat was buttoned wrong; but he looked like a man with the right and power to demand respect, no matter how he appeared before you and no matter what he did. His movements were clumsy but confident and self-reliant, his ways defied the usual conventions in human relations, but they were dignified and somewhat disdainful; his sharp metallic voice was wonderfully adapted to the radical judgments that he passed on persons and things. He always spoke in imperative words that would brook no contradiction and were made all the sharper by the almost painful impression of the tone which ran through everything he said. This tone expressed the firm conviction of his mission to dominate men's minds and prescribe them their laws. Before me stood the embodiment of a democratic dictator such as one might imagine in a daydream.

By 1847 the League of the Just became conscious of the need for a firmer theoretical foundation for their activities and decided to approach Marx and Engels, who were eager to enter the working-class movement in which they placed such high hopes. During two long Congresses in London the ideas of Marx were accepted in principle by the League, renamed the Communist League, and Marx was commissioned to set them down in a *Manifesto*. This classic document was scarcely drafted when it was overtaken by the 1848 revolutions.

1848: THE YEAR OF REVOLUTIONS

In France, the working-class National Guard turned against King Louis Philippe, who abdicated to make way for a provisional government of liberal tendencies with a more radical socialist wing. This government invited Marx back to Paris. He accepted the invitation all the more readily as the Belgian government had just expelled him for contravening his undertaking not to engage in political journalism. On his arrival in a Paris still littered with the debris of recent barricades, Marx opposed the current idea of a German workers' legion to liberate Germany: their task, he said, was to assist the revolution in Paris. By March, however, the revolution had reached Berlin and King Frederick William IV had been compelled to grant an elected Prussian parliament, a free press, and an Assembly to draw up a new Constitution. Marx immediately moved to Cologne and resumed his journalistic activities of five years before. The Communist League being more or less superfluous, Marx concentrated his energies during the following hectic year on the editorship of his new paper, the *Neue Rheinische Zeitung*.

In terms of circulation and impact the paper was a great success. It called itself an "organ of democracy" and advocated the two points of "a single, indivisible, democratic German republic, and war with Russia which would bring the restoration of Poland." During its first few months the paper made virtually no reference to working-class politics and concentrated on working for the emancipation of the bourgeoisie—a point of view which necessarily led to friction between Marx and the more radical artisan association in Cologne. By the autumn, the watershed of the revolution had passed: reaction triumphed in France and Austria, but Marx still favored an alliance with the more progressive elements of the bourgeoisie and refused to support separate working-class candidates for elections. His paper was encountering increasing difficulties with the authorities, but it was not until April 1849, a month before the collapse of the revolutionary movement, that Marx changed his tactics and advocated separate working-class political action. But it was far too late: the last number of the *Neue Rheinische Zeitung*, printed in red, appeared on May 18.

Marx returned once again to Paris, always optimistic: "a colossal eruption of the revolutionary crater was never more imminent than now in Paris," he wrote to Engels. But it was not to be. In July, the now familiar expulsion order arrived and in August 1849 he sailed for England to begin his long sleepless night of exile.

EXILE IN LONDON

Marx's fourth child was born soon after his arrival in England. Funds allowed the family only a few months of the comfortable life they were used to living; then came eviction which led them through a series of temporary lodgings to the three-room flat in Dean Street, Soho, where they stayed until 1856.

Marx was anticipating the outbreak of fresh revolutions in Europe and attempted to continue his journalistic activities by founding a monthly entitled *Neue-Rheinische Zeitung-Revue*. In it, Marx published a series of essays, later entitled *The Class Struggle in France*, in which he reconsidered the significance of the 1848 revolutions. He was also occupied by the activities of the Communist League, whose reconstituted London branch he had joined immediately on arrival. At first, Marx attempted a *rapprochement* with the Blanquists, but the reading that he had begun in the British Museum soon convinced him that "a new revolution is possible only in consequence of a new crisis." This led to a split with those in the Communist League who thought his attitude too quiescent. Engels departed to work for his father's firm in Manchester, and Marx soon retired from active politics. He belonged to no political organization for the next ten years.

The years in Dean Street were characterized by a constant lack of money. The fourth child, Guido, died in 1850 and another child the following year; but the worst blow to Marx was the death of his eldest son, aged eight, in 1856. Marx wrote to Engels: "My wife is ill, little Jenny is ill, Lenchen [the maid] has a sort of nervous fever. I could not and cannot call the doctor as I have no money for medicine. For 8–10 days I have fed the family on bread and potatoes and it is still questionable whether I can get any together today." Understandably, these domestic worries ground down Marx's naturally optimistic character: "There is no greater stupidity," he wrote to Engels, "than for people of general aspirations to marry and so surrender themselves to the small miseries of domestic and private life." It should be noted that Marx's income would have been quite adequate, had he known how to manage it carefully; but both he and Jenny had an extravagance (and generosity) that entailed continual financial crises. Marx was often to reflect that he, who wrote so much on capital, should have so little talent for managing it. The domestic situation was further complicated in 1851 by the birth of an illegitimate son to Helena Demuth, the German maid who had followed the family through all their peregrinations and was the only member of the household to have some domestic common sense. The father was Marx, but Engels (who had quite a reputation as a womanizer) agreed to accept paternity, the child was sent to foster care, and the whole matter hushed up.

A small legacy in 1856 enabled the family to rent a house in Haverstock Hill, but the necessity of keeping up the appropriate appearances soon brought back the trips to the pawnshop. Marx wrote in typical vein to Lassalle in 1861: "As far as my book is concerned, it will not be ready for two months. In order to avoid starvation during the last year I have had to do the most contemptible sorts of job and have often not been able to write a line of the stuff for months on end. In addition, it is characteristic of me that if I see something that I completed four weeks or so ago, I find it unsatisfactory and rework it completely." In the same year, Marx informed Engels of the repercussions of this on their family life: "My wife tells me every day that she wishes she were in the grave with the children and really I cannot hold it against her; for the humiliations, torments, and fears that we have to endure are in fact indescribable." It was not until 1864 that the death of his mother and a legacy from Wilhelm Wolff, an old communist comrade, brought substantial relief. But as financial worries receded, Marx's health deteriorated: like Job he was plagued by boils from head to foot. He dosed himself with such extraordinary medicines as creosote, opium, and arsenic, but the boils continued to debilitate him for years on end, and he could only comfort himself by reflecting that the bourgeoisie would have good cause to remember his sufferings from "this truly proletarian disease." Nevertheless—like many men

who appear intolerant in their professional capacities—
Marx had a very warm home life: he loved playing with
his children, and the week regularly culminated with a
Sunday picnic on Hampstead Heath accompanied by
singing and recitations from Shakespeare.

Marx's only regular source of income in the 1850s
(apart from Engels) was his articles for the *New York
Daily Tribune*, a radical paper with the largest circulation in America. These covered all aspects of contemporary politics and were highly regarded by the editor,
though Marx considered them merely an unwelcome
distraction from his main preoccupation—the drafting
of the work on economics for which he had originally
signed a contract in Paris in 1845. In spite of repeated
assertions that he was on the point of finishing, the work
made slow progress until the prospect of a crisis in 1857
impelled Marx to compose more than eight hundred
pages in less than six months. "I am working madly
through the nights," he wrote to Engels, "on a synthesis
of my economic studies, so that I at least have the main
principles clear before the deluge." This huge manuscript—which became known as the *Grundrisse* (outlines)—contained notes and excursuses for most of the
six parts in which Marx intended to publish the results
of his studies. However, Marx was only able to write up
the small introductory *Critique of Political Economy*
before he was enveloped in a time-consuming polemic
with Karl Vogt; and in the early 1860s he could only
amass more notes for the historical section of the first
part (notes subsequently published under the title
Theories of Surplus Value). This first part then ex-

panded into the three volumes of *Capital*—of which Marx only managed to complete the first, published in 1867—a work to which Marx declared himself to have "sacrificed health, happiness, and family." The other two volumes were left in manuscript to be edited by Engels after Marx's death. The other five parts were never even drafted.

THE LAST DECADE

One of the reasons why Marx's work on political economy was never finished was his involvement in the International Workingmen's Association, commonly known as the First International. In 1864 Marx was invited to an international meeting in St. Martin's Hall, London; here it was decided to found an International Workingmen's Association whose statutes and "Inaugural Address" were composed by Marx. During the next eight years Marx was the dominant personality on its General Council in London, drafting its various pronouncements on Continental movements, Polish independence as a bulwark against Russian barbarism, support for Irish Home Rule, the shortening of the working day, the transfer of land to common ownership, et cetera. This work took up the major part of Marx's time. In 1865 he wrote: "Compared with my work on the book [i.e., *Capital*] the International Association takes up an enormous amount of time, because I am in fact in charge of the whole business."

The most important political event in the lifetime of the International was the Franco-Prussian War and its aftermath. The stability that Europe had enjoyed after the 1848 revolutions was disturbed by the expansionist policy of Prussia under its "Iron Chancellor," Bismarck. In 1870 Bismarck provoked a war with France in which he very swiftly defeated and captured the Emperor Napoleon III. On behalf of the General Council of the International, Marx issued three addresses concerning the war: the first briefly supported the view that the war was one of defense from Germany's point of view and that a French defeat would bring about a revolution in France; the second criticized Prussia for continuing the war after the defeat of Bonaparte, declared that the Prussian annexation of Alsace and Lorraine only sowed the seeds of future war, and finally urged the Paris workers to support the Provisional government set up on the defeat of Bonaparte. The third address—much the longest, entitled *On the Civil War in France*—was written immediately following the bloody suppression of the rising of the Paris workers against the Provisional government, known as the Paris Commune. Two earlier drafts of this address survive.

The International was seriously weakened by the repression following the Commune, and as early as 1870 the split in its ranks—caused by the followers of Bakunin—was already becoming apparent. Insofar as they held any coherent doctrine, Bakunin's followers opposed any form of state, even a revolutionary workers' state, called for the equalization of classes, and proposed conspiratorial methods to attain these ends. By 1872 this quarrel had become so serious that Marx was compelled to bring the Association to an end by proposing the transfer of its seat to New York.

In 1869, Engels, who had already been subsidizing Marx to the tune of about £500 a year, decided to sell his partnership in the Manchester firm and so could settle an annuity on his friend. While retaining his revolutionary politics in the 1870s, Marx adopted more and more the life-style of a Victorian gentleman to which he had aspired during the two previous decades. Whereas before he had had to pawn "everything that was not nailed down" in order to keep up appearances in front of the visiting Lassalle, he could now send his daughters to a ladies' seminary, attend Continental spas for his health, and even boast of gambling on the stock exchange. The family now lived in a large house in Maitland Park Road, and Marx was able to play with the children of his two married daughters quite as boisterously as he had played with his own in Dean Street. But in spite of his freedom from financial and domestic worries, the spirit of creative synthesis that had so characterized his work during the two previous decades now deserted him. He had a sort of stroke in 1873 and spent a lot of time traveling in search of health. His work of the 1870s was therefore fragmentary, and he spent most of his working time in taking notes from his still enormous reading and on his wide correspondence. As well as working on the second edition of *Capital*, Volume One, and its French translation, Marx drew up a detailed criticism of the first common program of the German socialists who met at Gotha in 1875 at a congress which united the Lassallean wing with the Eisenach party led by Liebknecht and Bebel. These criticisms were published by Engels in

1891, under the title *Critique of the Gotha Programme*. Particularly in his later years, Marx began to be very interested in Russia, and among the correspondence of the last years of his life are letters containing a very balanced assessment of the possibilities of Russia's by-passing the capitalist stage of development and basing communism on existing peasant cooperatives.

The end of Marx's life was not a happy one. The death of his wife in 1881 robbed him of all enthusiasm for living, and in 1883 his daughter Jenny also died. Two months later, in March 1883, Marx died in his arm-chair.

The Thought

THE EARLY WRITINGS

The early writings of Marx are those composed in Germany and Paris up to, and including, 1844. It was not until the composition of *The German Ideology*—in Brussels in 1845–46—that Marx arrived at the materialistic conception of history that was to be the "guiding thread" for the rest of his studies. During these early years, Marx's writings show a development through the successive stages of idealism—romantic and then Hegelian—to liberal rationalism and an extended criticism of Hegel's philosophy. Engels said that Marx's ideas were based on a synthesis of German idealist philosophy, French political theory, and English classical economics: the early writ-

ings show Marx assimilating all three influences—
though not, as yet, integrating them.

The intellectual background of Marx's home and
school was the rationalism of the Enlightenment, a
pale Protestantism incorporating the virtues of reason,
moderation, and hard work. A radically different perspective was opened up by Baron von Westphalen.
Marx's daughter Eleanor wrote that the Baron "filled
Karl Marx with enthusiasm for the romantic school and,
whereas his father read Voltaire and Racine with him,
the Baron read him Homer and Shakespeare—who remained his favorite authors all his life." In Bonn, therefore, Marx gave himself up to the current romanticism,
though Berlin brought about a decisive change: previously, Hegel's conceptual rationalism had been rejected
by Marx, the follower of Kant and Fichte, the romantic
subjectivist who considered the highest being to be
separate from earthly reality. Now, however, it began
to appear to him as though the idea was immanent in
the real. Previously, Marx had "read fragments of Hegel's
philosophy, but I did not care for its grotesque and
rocky melody." Now he embraced Hegelianism in a con-
version that was as profound as it was sudden. It was
probably the most important intellectual step of his
whole life. For however much he was to criticize Hegel,
accuse him of idealism, and try to stand his dialectic
"on its feet," Marx was the first to admit that his
method stemmed directly from that of his master of
the 1830s.

Hegel started from the belief that, as he said of the
French Revolution, "man's existence has its center in

his head, i.e., in Reason, under whose inspiration he builds up the world of reality." In his greatest work, *The Phenomenology of Spirit*, Hegel traced the development of mind, or spirit, reintroducing historical movement into philosophy and asserting that the human mind can attain to absolute knowledge. He analyzed the development of human consciousness from its immediate perception of the here and now to the stage of self-consciousness, the understanding that allowed man to analyze the world and order his own actions accordingly. Following this was the stage of reason itself, understanding of the real, after which spirit, by means of religion and art, attained to absolute knowledge, the level at which man recognized in the world the stages of his own reason. These stages Hegel called "alienations," insofar as they were creations of the human mind yet thought of as independent and superior to the human mind. This absolute knowledge was at the same time a sort of recapitulation of the human spirit, for each successive stage retained elements of the previous ones at the same time as it went beyond them. This movement that suppressed and yet conserved Hegel called *Aufhebung*, a word that has this double sense in German. Hegel also talked of "the power of the negative," thinking that there was always a tension between any present state of affairs and what it was becoming. For any present state of affairs was in the process of being negated, changed into something else. This process was what Hegel meant by dialectic.

Hegel's philosophy was ambivalent: although he himself preferred to talk of philosophy painting gray with gray and the owl of Minerva only rising at dusk, emphasis on its negative and dialectic side could obviously give it a radical bent—a development associated with a group of intellectuals known as the Young Hegelians. They embarked on a process of secularization, progressing from a critique of religion to one of politics and society. It is important to note that Marx in his early writings worked at his ideas in interaction with the other members of this close-knit movement. His doctoral thesis clearly reflected the Young Hegelian climate: its field—post-Aristotelian Greek philosophy—was one of general interest to the Young Hegelians and Marx's proclamation in the Preface that "Philosophy makes no secret of it. Prometheus' confession 'in a word, I detest all Gods,' is its own confession, its own slogan against all Gods in heaven and earth who do not recognize man's self-consciousness as the highest divinity," was typical of the Young Hegelians' antireligious idealism. The way forward for Marx lay in an application to the "real" world of the principles that Hegel had discovered.

But Marx did not immediately have the leisure to work on this line of thought: deprived of the possibility of an academic career, his contact with the real world came through his work as a journalist for the *Rheinische Zeitung*. In his seven major articles for the paper, he seldom made his own ideas explicit, since he gave his articles the form of critical exegesis by exposing the absurdities in his opponents' ideas. For this he used any weapon to hand, usually combining a radical Hegelianism with the simple rationalism of the Enlightenment. In October 1842, now an editor, Marx had to reply to the accusation that his paper was flirting with communist ideas. "The *Rheinische Zeitung*," he wrote, "does not even concede theoretical validity to communist ideas in their present form, let alone desires their practical realization"; and he promised a fundamental criticism of such ideas. Soon, however, Marx had to write on such sociopolitical matters as the law on the thefts of wood and the poverty of the Moselle winegrowers—subjects, as he said later, which "provided the first occasions for occupying myself with economic questions" and impressed on him how closely the laws were formed by the interests of those who were in power.

The eighteen months following the suppression of the *Rheinische Zeitung* were to be decisive for Marx's ideas: in his assault on the metaphysical fog that engulfed not only Hegel but also much Young Hegelian writing, Marx was helped by two things. First, he was reading a lot of politics and history: he read French socialism even before he went to Paris and his reading on the French Revolution was extensive. Indeed, his writing of this period can be viewed as an extended meditation on the question of why the French Revolution, which started out with such excellent principles, had yet failed to solve the fundamental problem of the redistribution of social wealth. Second, there was the influence of Ludwig Feuerbach. Although Engels exaggerated when he said later that "we all became Feuerbachians," this influence was profound. Feuerbach was fundamentally interested in religion, and his main thesis was that God was merely a projection of human attributes, desires, and potentialities. If men once realized this, they would be in a position to appropriate these attributes for themselves by realizing that they had created God, not God them, and thus be in a position to restore to themselves their alienated "species-being" or communal essence. What interested Marx was the application of this approach to Hegel's philosophy, which Feuerbach regarded as the last bulwark of theology, in that Hegel still started from the ideal instead of the real. Feuerbach wrote: "The true relationship of thought to being is this: being is the subject, thought the predicate. Thought arises from being—being does not arise from thought."

This view of Feuerbach was incorporated into a long manuscript that Marx composed in the summer of 1843. Here, by means of a critique of Hegel, Marx's views on democracy and the abolition of the State began to take shape. According to Hegel's political philosophy, human consciousness manifested itself objectively in man's juridical, social, and political institutions which alone permitted man to attain to full liberty. Only the highest level of social organization—the State—was capable of uniting particular rights and universal reason. Hegel thus rejected the view that man was free by nature: on the contrary, for him the State was the only means of making man's freedom real. In other words, Hegel was aware of the social problems created by a competitive society in which there was an economic war of all against all—a state of affairs which he summed up under the term "Civil Society"; but he considered that these conflicts could be harmonized by the organs of the State into some "higher" unity. Following Feuerbach, Marx's fundamental criticism of Hegel was that, as in religion men had imagined God to be the creator and man to be dependent on Him, so Hegel mistakenly started from the Idea of the State and made everything else—the family and various social groups—dependent on this Idea. Applying this general approach to particular issues, Marx declared himself in favor of democracy: "Just as religion does not create man, but man creates religion, so the constitution does not create the people but the people the constitution." Marx was especially concerned, in a few pages of brilliant analysis, to reject Hegel's view that the bureaucracy performed a mediating function between different social groups and thus acted as a "universal class" in the interests of all. Marx considered that bureaucracy encouraged the political divisions that were essential to its own existence and thus pursued its own ends to the detriment of the community at large. Toward the end of his manuscript, Marx described how he expected universal suffrage to inaugurate the reform of civil society by bringing back to it the social essence of man as a communal being that had been stolen from him and transferred to the sphere of constitutions that had no effect on his real life.

The manuscript on Hegel was never published, but the embryonic ideas it contained received a clearer formulation when Marx got to Paris. During the winter of 1843–44 Marx wrote two essays for the *Deutsch-französische Jahrbücher*—both as clear and sparkling as the Hegel manuscript had been involved and obscure. In the first, entitled "On the Jewish Question," Marx reviewed the opinions of his old mentor Bruno Bauer on Jewish emancipation. According to Bauer, for Jewish emancipation to be effective, the state had to cease to be Christian—otherwise discrimination against the Jews was inevitable. But for Marx, Bauer had not gone far enough: the mere secularization of politics did not entail the emancipation of men as human beings. The United States had no established religion, yet was notorious for the religiosity of its inhabitants. "But since the existence of religion," Marx continued, "is the existence of a defect, the source of this defect can only be sought in the *nature* of the state itself. Religion for us no longer has the force of a basis for secular deficiencies but only that of a phenomenon. We do not change secular questions into theological ones. We change theological questions into secular ones. History has for long enough been resolved into superstition: we now resolve superstition into history. The question of the *relationship* between political emancipation and religion becomes for us a question of the relationship of political emancipation to human emancipation." In Marx's view this problem arose because "man has a life both in the political community, where he is valued as a communal being, and in civil society, where he is active as a private individual, treats other men as means, degrades himself to a means, and becomes the plaything of alien powers."

Bauer had argued for a state based exclusively on the universal rights of man as proclaimed by the French Revolution and the American Declaration of Independence. For Marx, however, the rights of man were only the rights of the atomized, mutually hostile individuals of civil society. Thus "the right of man to freedom is not based on the union of man with man, but on the separation of man from man. . . . The right of man to property is the right to enjoy his possessions and dispose of the same arbitrarily, without regard for other men, independently of society, the right of selfishness. It is the former individual freedom together with its latter application that forms the basis of civil society. It leads man to see in other men not the realization but the limitation of his own freedom."

After pointing out that the society inaugurated by the French Revolution had forfeited many of the social and communal dimensions present in feudal society, Marx sketched his goal of bridging the gap between the individual viewed as a citizen member of a community and as an isolated egoistic member of civil society: "Human emancipation will only be complete when the real, individual man has absorbed into himself the abstract citizen; when as an individual man, in his everyday life, in his work, and in his individual relationships, he has become a *species-being*; and when he has recognized and organized his own powers (*forces propres*) and *social* powers so that he no longer separates this social power from himself as political power."

The article "On the Jewish Question" had set the goal of full human emancipation; in his second article for the *Jahrbücher* Marx identified the means to achieve it. This article was intended as an introduction to his critique of Hegel which was to be written up for publication. The article began with Marx's famous epigrams on religion: "The foundation of irreligious criticism is this: man makes religion, religion does not make man. But man is no abstract being squatting outside the world.

Man is the world of man, the state, society. This state, this society, produces religion's inverted attitude to the world, because they are an inverted world themselves. Thus the struggle against religion is indirectly the struggle against that world whose spiritual aroma is religion. . . . Religion is the sigh of the oppressed creature, the feeling of a heartless world, and the soul of soulless circumstances. It is the opium of the people. . . ." But the role of religion having been exposed, the duty of philosophers was now to direct their attention to politics, a particularly appropriate activity in a Germany which was, according to Marx, still pre-1789. The one hope for Germany lay in her political philosophy, which was very progressive: the Germans had *thought* what other nations had *done*. Therefore, to criticize this philosophy and progress beyond it would show, at least theoretically, what the future of society was to be. And although Marx was clear that "the criticism of religion ends with the doctrine that man is the highest being for man, that is, with the categorical imperative to overthrow all circumstances in which man is humiliated, enslaved, abandoned, and despised," the difficulty obviously lay in finding "a passive element, a material basis" necessary to revolution. He proclaimed the solution in a passage that has given much support to the view of Marx as a messianic, prophetic figure. The solution lay

in the formation of a class with radical chains, a class in civil society that is not a class of civil society, of a social group that is the dissolution of all social groups, of a sphere that has a universal character because of its universal sufferings and lays claim to no particular right, because it is the object of no particular injustice but of injustice in general. This class can no longer lay claim to a historical status, but only to a human one. It is, finally, a sphere that cannot emancipate itself without emancipating these other spheres themselves. In a word, it is the complete loss of humanity and thus can only recover itself by a complete redemption of humanity. This dissolution of society, as a particular class, is the proletariat. . . .

Thus the vehicle of revolution was clear to Marx: the proletariat was destined to assume the universal role that Hegel had misleadingly assigned to the bureaucracy. But hitherto Marx's writings had been almost exclusively political, although he had come to realize that politics was not enough: his interest in the essential economic dimension was sparked by an essay published in the *Deutsch-französische Jahrbücher* alongside his own two. It was by Engels and entitled "Outlines of a Critique of Political Economy." In it, Engels indicted private property and its concomitant spirit of competition. Growing capitalist accumulation necessarily entailed a lowering of salaries and accentuated the class struggle. Uncurtailed growth of the economy meant recurrent crises, and the progress of science only served to increase the misery of the workers. This "sketch of genius" (as he later called it) made a great impression on Marx, and his notebooks during the summer of 1844 begin with extracts from it. These notes (unpublished by Marx) were entitled by their first editors "Economic

and Philosophical Manuscripts" (EPM) and represent
a radical critique of capitalism based partly on Engels,
partly on the anti-industrial ideas of such German
romantics as Schiller, and partly on Feuerbach's humanism. On their first full publication in 1932 they were
hailed by some as Marx's most important single piece
of work (see Chapter iii, p. 86).

The EPM consist of three main sections: a critique of
the classical economists culminating with a section on
alienated labor; a description of communism; and a
critique of Hegel's dialectic.

The first section contains lengthy quotations from the
classical economists—in particular Adam Smith and
David Ricardo—to demonstrate the increasing polarization of classes and the deleterious effects of private
property. Although he considered that the economists
faithfully reported the workings of capitalist society,
Marx criticized their approach on three main grounds:
first, while admitting that labor was fundamental to the
working of the economy, they acquiesced in assigning to
it an increasingly poverty-stricken role; second, they did
not view the economic system as one of interacting
forces, that is, they took the laws of capitalism to be
immutable and could not explain the origins of the
system they were describing; and third, they took a one-
sided view of man simply as a cog in the economic
wheel and did not consider him "in his free time, as a
human being."

At this point Marx began a new section headed
"alienated labor" and containing a description of the
general impoverishment and dehumanization of the

worker in capitalist society. Alienated labor had four aspects to it. First, the worker was related to the product of his labor as to an alien object; it stood over and above him, opposed to him as an independent power. Second, the worker became alienated from himself in the very act of production; the worker did not view his work as part of his real life and did not feel at home in it. Third, man's "species-life," his social essence, was taken away from him in his work which did not represent the harmonious efforts of man as a "species-being." Fourth, man found himself alienated from other men.

In an extended note on James Mill written about this time (unfortunately not included in most editions of the EPM), Marx attacked the notion of credit, which he called "the economic judgment on the morality of a man. In credit, man himself, instead of metal or paper, has become the mediator of exchange but not as man, but as the existence of capital and interest." In contemporary society, according to Marx, men were increasingly producing with the sole object of exchanging and thus "you have no relation to my object as a human being because I myself have no human relation to it . . . our mutual value is the value of our objects for us." The passage toward the end of the note constitutes a sort of positive counterpart to the description of alienated labor and deserves quoting in full:

> Supposing that we had produced in a human manner; each of us would in his production have doubly affirmed himself and his fellow men. I would have: (1) objectified in my production my individuality and its peculiarity and thus both in

my activity enjoyed an individual expression of my
life and also in looking at the object have had the
individual pleasure of realizing that my personality was objective, visible to the senses and thus a
power raised beyond all doubt. (2) In your enjoyment of use of my product I would have had the
direct enjoyment of realizing that I had both satis-
fied a human need by my work and also objectified
the human essence and therefore fashioned for
another human being the object that met his need.
(3) I would have been for you the mediator between you and the species and thus been acknowl-
edged and felt by you as a completion of your own
essence and a necessary part of yourself and have
thus realized that I am confirmed both in your
thought and in your love. (4) In my expression of
my life I would have fashioned your expression of
your life, and thus in my own activity have realized
my own essence, my human, my communal essence.

The second main section of the EPM contained Marx's
solution to the problem of alienation in communism.
Although while still in Germany he had rejected communism as a "dogmatic and one-sided abstraction," the
impact of Paris had made him a swift convert. But
Marx's communism was not the "crude" kind, inspired
by "universal envy," that aimed to negate all culture in
a leveling-down process. He summarized his ideas in an
almost mystical passage:

. . . communism as the positive abolition of private
property and thus of human self-alienation and
therefore the real reappropriation of the human

essence by and for man. This is communism as the complete and conscious return of man himself as a social, i.e., human being. Communism as completed naturalism is humanism and as completed humanism is naturalism. It is the genuine solution of the antagonism between man and nature and between man and man. It is the true solution of the struggle between existence and essence, between objectification and self-affirmation, between freedom and necessity, between individual and species. It is the solution to the riddle of history and knows itself to be this solution.

In the following sections (in many ways the key passage of the EPM), Marx expanded on three particular aspects of his conception of communism. First, he stressed that communism was a *historical* phenomenon whose genesis was "the entire movement of history." At the present stage, the essential problem was an economic one—in particular, the abolition of private property: "the positive abolition of private property and the appropriation of human life is the positive abolition of all alienation, thus the return of man from religion, family, state, etc., to his human, that is, social being." Second, Marx stressed that everything about man—starting with his language—was *social*. Even man's relationship to nature was included in this social dimension: "thus society completes the essential unity of man with nature, it is the genuine resurrection of nature, the fulfilled naturalism of man and humanism of nature. . . . For not only the five senses but also the so-called spiritual and moral senses (will, love, etc.), in a word, human love and the humanity of the senses come into being only through the existence of their object, through nature humanized. The development of the five senses is a labor of the whole previous history of the world." Nevertheless, Marx emphasized, thirdly, that the stress on man's social aspects only served to enhance the *individuality* of communist, unalienated man, whom he described as "total" or "all-sided." For just as the state of alienation vitiated all human faculties, so the supersession of this alienation would be a total liberation. It would not just be limited to the possession and enjoyment of material objects: all human faculties would, in their different ways, become means of appropriating reality. This was difficult to imagine for alienated man, since private property had so blunted men's sensibility that they could only imagine an object to be theirs when they actually possessed it: all physical and intellectual senses had been replaced by the single alienation of *having*. And, finally, the reciprocal relationship between man and nature would be reflected in a single all-embracing science: "natural science will in time comprise the science of man, as the science of man will embrace natural science: there will be one single science."

The third and final section of the EPM was devoted to a critique of Hegel's dialectic as found in his most famous work, *The Phenomenology of Spirit*. Marx began by praising Feuerbach for having shown that Hegel's philosophy was no more than a rationalized theology and discovering the true materialist approach by starting from the social relationship of man to man. But Marx's attitude to Hegel was far from being wholly negative: "The greatness of Hegel's *Phenomenology* and its final product, the dialectic of negativity as the moving and creating principle, is on the one hand that Hegel conceives of the self-creation of man as a process, objectification as loss of the object, as externalization and the transcendence of this externalization. This means, therefore, that he grasps the nature of labor and understands objective man, true because real man, as the result of his own labor." On the other hand, this whole dialectic was viewed from an idealist standpoint: "The appropriation of man's objectified and alienated faculties is thus first only an appropriation that occurs in the mind, in pure thought, i.e., in abstraction." Marx, however, started from the "real man of flesh and blood, standing on the solid round earth and breathing in and out all the powers of nature" and defined his position as a consistent naturalism or humanism that avoided both idealism and materialism. Hegel saw man as a disembodied consciousness and the world as necessarily inimical to man's fulfillment, but Marx considered that it was only man's present relationship to the world that was askew: man needed to interact with external objects in order to develop or "objectify" himself. For Hegel, all objectification was alienation; for Marx, man could overcome alienation only if he objectified himself by using nature in cooperation with his fellow men.

With his move to Brussels in 1845, Marx's writings take on a systematic form—albeit as an open-ended system—that is not present in his early writings. These early writings document Marx's struggle to conclude, from very idealistic beginnings, that the fundamental activity of man was one of productive interchange with nature; that this activity was vitiated by the class divisions of capitalist society with its institutions of private property and the division of labor; and that this present alienation could be overcome by a proletarian revolution inaugurating communism.

HISTORY

The fact that Marx never used the expression "historical materialism" (still less "dialectical materialism") is not merely a linguistic point: it indicates the open-ended nature of his approach to history, which he preferred to call "the materialist conception of history." The key to this approach was the idea (central to the EPM) that the essential element in an understanding of man and his history was a comprehension of man's productive activity. The fundamental activity of man was the way he obtained his means of subsistence by interaction with nature—in short, his labor. Marx summed up in *Capital* his view of labor as the instrument of man's self-creation: "Labor is a process in which both man and nature participate, and in which man of his own accord starts, regulates, and controls the material reactions between himself and nature. . . . By thus acting on the external world and changing it, he at the same time changes his own nature. He develops his slumbering powers and compels them to act in obedience to his sway." This self-creation through labor was the primary factor in history, and the ideas and concepts—political, philosophical, or religious—

through which men interpreted this activity were secondary. History was not the result of accident, nor was it shaped by the acts of great men (still less by supernatural powers): history was the—mostly unconscious—creation of laboring men, and it was subject to observable laws.

Perhaps the most vital point in any understanding of Marx is that when he called himself a materialist he meant quite simply that in order to understand man it was essential to begin with the material conditions of his production. Thus Marx was not an empiricist: he did not believe that insight could be gained from a collection of dead facts; he drew a distinction between essence and appearance; and he poured considerable scorn on "common sense," which he considered as poor a guide in history and economics as it would be to the question of whether the earth moved around the sun. Nor was Marx a materialist in the rather metaphysical sense of someone who believes that the world consists only of matter. Indeed, Marx's most detailed account of his materialist conception of history was contained in *The German Ideology*, which was intended to distinguish his views from those of Feuerbach on precisely this question. His main point—summarized trenchantly in the accompanying *Theses on Feuerbach*—was that man was *not* simply a product of material conditions: such a view left out the subjective, creative side of man's interaction with nature. Taking to task the French materialists of the eighteenth century, Marx wrote that "the materialist doctrine concerning the changing of circumstances and upbringing forgets that circumstances are made by men and the educator must himself be educated." What Marx was concerned centrally to deny was the validity of any doctrine that claimed to be able to give an "objective," neutral, or static account of the world from an uninvolved position. Thus "the question whether objective truth can be attributed to human thinking is not a question of theory but a *practical* question." In order to attain to this "neutral" view a man would have to be outside society—just as Archimedes' firm point from which to start his system of levers would have had to be outside the world. But no one could get outside society, no more than Archimedes could get outside the world. Since, therefore, everyone spoke from a point of view, the eleventh, and best-known, *Thesis* was mandatory on all: "Philosophers have only *interpreted* the world, in various ways; the point is to *change* it."

There are in the later Marx certain traces of positivism and he was certainly not immune to the general enthusiasm for a supposedly value-free natural science that reached its high point in late Victorian society. But the general view (obviously derived from Hegel) that no element in the total process of history could be isolated and given a significance unaffected by the other elements—this view stayed with Marx throughout his life.

Marx's ideas are often referred to as offering "the economic interpretation of history." The clearest statement of the importance Marx attached to economics is contained in the Preface to the *Critique of Political Economy*. Here Marx stated:

In the social production of their life, men enter
into definite relations that are indispensable and
independent of their will, relations of production
which correspond to a definite state of development
of their material productive forces. The sum total
of these relations of production constitutes the economic structure of society, the real foundation, on
which rises a legal and political superstructure and
to which correspond definite forms of social consciousness. The mode of production of material
life conditions the social, political, and intellectual
life process in general. It is not the consciousness
of men that determines their being, but, on the contrary, their social being that determines their consciousness. At a certain stage of their development,
the material productive forces of society come in
conflict with the existing relations of production,
or—what is but a legal expression for the same
thing—with the property relations within which
they have been at work hitherto. From forms of
development of the productive forces these relations turn into their fetters. Then begins an epoch
of social revolution.

There were, of course, elements in Marx's thought
that tended to overemphasize aspects of necessity and
predetermination in his view of society. Engels wrote
later: "Marx and I are ourselves partly to blame for the
fact that the younger people sometimes lay more stress
on the economic side than is due to it. We had to emphasize the main principle vis-à-vis our adversaries, who
denied it, and we had not always the time, the place, or
the opportunity to give their due to the other elements

involved in the interaction." In consequence, some interpreters have read into the passage from Marx quoted above a kind of economic determinism, supposing him to have said that other elements in the historical process were uniquely determined by the economic one; or even that the only important economic factor was the actual instruments of production. It is true that Marx sometimes narrowed down the determining factor in such statements as "the hand mill will give you a society with the feudal lord, the steam engine a society with the industrial capitalist." It has been strongly argued in criticism of Marx that any theory of historical materialism that separates the base from the superstructure is invalid, since the base necessarily involves elements from the superstructure—for example, it is impossible to conceive of any economic organization of society without some concept of rules and obligations. But it is doubtful whether Marx ever formulated his theory as the strict causal one implied by this criticism. The most that could be said is that for Marx technological change was a necessary, though not a sufficient, condition of social change. Nor is the language used to describe the relationship of the base to the superstructure always precise: sometimes Marx uses the term "determine," sometimes the milder "condition," sometimes again the phrase "correspond to"—which conveys a rather different idea. Thus Marx's theory is best regarded as intended to supply a series of flexible structural concepts through which to interpret the development of past and present societies.

It is also clear that Marx assigned a positive role to

noneconomic factors in society. Indeed, he sometimes
included the workers themselves among the instruments
of production and even called the revolutionary class
"the greatest productive power of all the instruments of
production." It is significant that in the quotation above
from the Preface what is said to determine consciousness is not simply "being" but "*social* being." Yet ideas,
for Marx, were definitely of secondary importance in the
understanding of society. He warned that just as we
would be chary of judging an individual by what he
thought of himself, so we should not rely on the self-
interpretation of a particular epoch. To take a particular
example: the rights of man as proclaimed in the French
Revolution and the Constitution of the United States
were not eternal truths about the nature of man which
happened to be discovered at that particular time—as
those who proclaimed them imagined; they could be
fully undestood only if viewed in the context of demands
by new commercial groups for the end of feudal re-
strictions and for free competition in economic affairs.
It was in this sense of ideas propagated to serve a particular class interest that Marx usually used the term
"ideology."

Marx would have been the first to agree that his own
ideas were in some sense ideological in that they, too,
were destined to serve a class interest. But he would
have equally insisted that although his ideas could not
claim objective and static truth, they were nevertheless
valid in terms of the point of view from which they
stemmed and which they articulated—that of the proletariat. This position throws some light on the difficult

question of whether Marx's views imply an ethical standpoint. The answer (though not a very satisfactory one for those who believe in a sharp distinction between fact and value) is that Marx does have an ethical standpoint, but not one that one can describe in isolation from his statements on society and history. For example, Marx *does* have a concept of human nature—but not a static one which, as in many previous political philosophers, would act as an easy yardstick from which to read off recommendations about society. Marx's laboring, productive man is constantly developing and changing his relationship to the world and thereby changing—creating—his own nature.

This self-creation of man (albeit under determined circumstances) is central for Marx. Thus the instruments of production can never be isolated from their social context. The core of the Marxian dialectic is the unity of subjective and objective factors that is present, to some extent, throughout history and increasingly so as the revolution approaches. "History does nothing; it does not possess immense riches, it does not fight battles. It is men, real, living men, who do all this, who possess things and fight battles. It is not 'history' which uses men as a means of achieving—as if it were an individual person—its own ends. History is nothing but the activity of men in pursuit of their ends." Or again: "Men make their own history, but they do not make it just as they please; they do not make it under circumstances chosen by themselves, but under circumstances directly encountered, given, and transmitted from the past."

The most important concept in Marx that mediated

the subjective and objective sides of the dialectic was that of class. Classes were the basic social groups by means of whose conflict society developed in accordance with changes in its economic substructure. The opening words of *The Communist Manifesto* were: "The history of all hitherto existing societies is the history of class struggles." Unfortunately, Marx nowhere offers a systematic analysis of the concept of class. But it is clear that the role played by classes is a compound of subjective and objective factors.

On the objective side, an obvious question is: how many classes are there? There is the beginning of an answer at the end of *Capital*, Volume Three, where Marx stated that, in terms of identity of revenues and sources of revenue, there were three great social classes—wage-laborers, capitalists, and landowners; but the manuscript broke off just as Marx was putting the crucial question as to why doctors, lawyers, et cetera, were not therefore separate classes. Marx often used a model consisting of only two classes: this model is present in *The Communist Manifesto*, where Marx wrote that "society as a whole is more and more splitting up into two great classes directly facing each other: bourgeoisie and proletariat": and the same view reappears in *Capital*. Here the criterion for belonging to a class is ownership or nonownership of the means of production. It should be emphasized (particularly when discussing the two-class models) that Marx was thinking in terms of trends and projected into the future tendencies he saw in contemporary society. One of the most important of these trends was the impoverishment of the proletariat. Marx was usually chary of claiming that the proletariat would become immiserized in any absolute sense. Such an idea would not have harmonized well with his view of all human needs as mediated through society. What he did claim was that the gap in resources between those who owned the means of production and those who did not would widen.

In contemporary comment Marx applied the term "class" to several social groups. In Britain, Marx talked of "the ruling classes," and he even went so far as to say that finance capitalists and industrial capitalists "form two distinct classes." At the other end of the social scale was what Marx called the *Lumpenproletariat*, whom he described as "a recruiting ground for thieves and criminals of all kinds, living on the crumbs of society, people without a definite trade, vagabonds, people without a hearth or a home." In other words, the *Lumpenproletariat* were the drop-outs of society who had no stake in the development of society and so no historical role to play—except occasionally to sell their services to the bourgeoisie. A particular problem for the two-class model was the peasantry. Although Marx's normal characterization of the proletariat applied only to industrial workers, yet sometimes he spoke of the proletariat as comprising the vast majority of the people in capitalist society and so, presumably, as including farm laborers; in a comment on Bakunin in 1875 he spoke of the possibility of a situation in which "the capitalist tenant has ousted the peasants, and the real tiller of the soil is just as much a proletarian, a wage worker, as is the urban worker and thus shares with him interests that are directly the same." He also, in the same comment, said that sometimes even the landowning peasant belongs to the proletariat, though he is not conscious of it: the burden of mortgage on his land means that he does not really own it and is, in effect, working for someone else. Thus if the peasants are held to be proletarians and the landowners to be capitalists, the two-class model is again in force. There are also indications in some of Marx's later unpublished writings that he took into account the growth of the middle classes and the increasing importance in society of the service industries—but he did not give these factors any systematic treatment.

Equally important in Marx's view of class was the subjective or dynamic element: a class existed only when it was conscious of itself as such, and this always implied common hostility to another social group. Marx was sometimes hesitant as to whether even the capitalists formed a class in the full sense of the word. He wrote of them: "the separate individuals form a class insofar as they have to carry on a common battle against another class; otherwise they are on hostile terms with each other as competitors." The same applied to the proletariat: Marx spoke of times when "the proletariat is not yet sufficiently developed to constitute itself into a class," and said of the proletariat that "this mass is already a class in opposition to capital, but not yet a class for itself." In *The Communist Manifesto* he declared, "this organization of the proletarians into a class, and consequently into a political party, is continually being upset again by the competition between the workers themselves": and as late as 1866 Marx talked of the

International as an instrument for "the organization of the workers into a class." The clearest account of the subject element in class is Marx's description of the French peasantry: "Insofar as millions of families live under economic conditions of existence that separate their mode of life, their interests, and their culture from those of the other classes and put them in hostile opposition to the latter, they form a class. Insofar as there is merely a local interconnection among those small-holding peasants and the identity of their interests begets no community, no national bond, and no political organization among them, they do not form a class. They are consequently incapable of enforcing their class interest in their own name. ... ."

Engels once advised a correspondent who had inquired about historical materialism to read Marx's comments on contemporary history such as *The Eighteenth Brumaire*. In order to stress the flexibility of Marx's approach to history it is worth considering in rather more detail two "case studies": his comments on the relation of art to socioeconomic factors, and the possible future development of Russian society.

At the end of the General Introduction to the *Grundrisse*, Marx noted a number of points that he intended to deal with later; one of these was "the unequal relation between the development of material production and art, for instance." In other words, "certain periods of the highest development of art stand in no direct connection to the general development of society, or to the material basis and skeleton structure of its organization." For example, Greek mythology was the basis of Greek art; but the view of nature and social relations which had shaped Greek imagination and art was not possible in an age of automatic machinery, locomotives, and electricity. What, asked Marx, became of the Goddess Fama when faced with Printing House Square? Or how was Achilles possible side by side with powder and lead? Thus the problem was in understanding why Greek art "still constitutes for us a source of aesthetic enjoyment and in certain respects prevails as the standard and model beyond attainment." Marx's answer to this question was: "Why should the childhood of human society, where it has obtained its most beautiful development, not exert an eternal charm as an age that will never return?" This answer is certainly unsatisfactory, but the discussion shows that Marx was well aware that his theory could not necessarily yield any ready-made answers to historical problems.

The second example is Marx's view of Russian development. In 1877, Mikhailovsky, one of the leading Russian Populist theoreticians, attacked Marx's ideas by claiming that *Capital* involved a condemnation of the efforts of Russians who worked for a development in their country which would bypass the capitalist stage. In reply, Marx insisted on the possibility of Russia's avoiding the capitalist stage and attacked Mikhailovsky, who "absolutely must metamorphose my historical sketch of the genesis of capitalism in Western Europe into a historico-philosophical theory of the general path every people is fated to tread, whatever the historical circumstances in which it finds itself . . ." and criticized any approach which tried to understand history "by

using as one's master key a general historico-philosophical theory, the supreme virtue of which consists in being
supra-historical."

Marx returned to this question in 1881 when the
Russian Marxist Vera Sassoulitch asked him to clarify
his views:

> Lately [she wrote] we often hear it said that the
> rural commune is an archaic form condemned to
> perish by history, scientific socialism and all that
> is least subject to debate. The people who preach
> this call themselves your disciples *par excellence*:
> "Marxists." The strongest of their arguments is
> often: "Marx has said it." "But how do you deduce
> it from his *Capital*? He does not discuss the
> agrarian problem nor Russia," was the objection.
> Your disciples reply: "He would have said it had
> he talked of our country."

Marx's short reply was enigmatic:

> The analysis given in *Capital* does not offer any
> reasons either for or against the vitality of the
> rural commune, but the special study that I have
> made of it, for which I have researched the ma-
> terial in its original sources, has convinced me that
> this commune is the starting point for the social
> regeneration of Russia, but that, in order for it to
> function as such, it would be necessary first of all
> to eliminate the deleterious influences that assail
> it on all sides and then to assure it the normal con-
> ditions for a spontaneous development.

Brief though Marx's reply was, it was based on three
very lengthy drafts which thoroughly analyzed the de-

velopment of the peasant commune and contained the more optimistic conclusion that:

> To save the Russian commune, a Russian revolution is necessary. Moreover, the Russian Government and the "new pillars of society" are doing their best to prepare the masses for such a catastrophe. If the revolution comes at an opportune moment, if it concentrates all its forces to ensure the free development of the rural commune, this commune will soon develop into an element that regenerates Russian society and guarantees superiority over countries enslaved by the capitalist regime.

Thus Marx's view on this question so crucial to the development of Marxism was fatefully ambivalent.

These two case studies illustrate the flexibility of Marx's approach to history—an approach that was always informed by the dialectical unity of subjective and objective factors that lay at the center of his views.

ECONOMICS

In his best-known formulation of the materialist conception of history, Marx wrote that "in the social production of their life, men enter into definite relations that are indispensable and independent of their will, relations of production which correspond to a definite stage of development of their material productive forces." Marx's economic doctrines are embedded in this conception of history in that they aim to analyze the relations of production and corresponding material productive forces in bourgeois society—"to lay bare the economic law of modern society," as he wrote in the Preface to *Capital*. That Marx's economics cannot be separated from his sociology, his politics, or his history can be seen from *Capital* itself, whose first volume is by no means as dryly economic as is sometimes thought: more than half the book is an extremely readable application of the materialist conception of history to British capitalism in his day. The wealth of detail and vividness of style demonstrate both the meticulousness of his research and his great literary talent. Nevertheless, as Marx himself said, every beginning is difficult and *Capital* is no exception. Before offering a brief description of Marx's main economic doctrines a few remarks on the nature of Marx's approach are necessary—all the more so as much interest has focused recently on Marx's methodology.

The two main places where Marx describes his method are the "General Introduction" to the *Grundrisse* and the Preface to the second edition of *Capital*. These passages are also crucial for an understanding of what Marx owed to Hegel. Marx says here that the researcher begins by having before him the chaotic mass of his subject matter—in this case modern bourgeois society. He then breaks it down into its constituent elements and arrives at ever more simple and abstract concepts, each of which, however, only has full meaning by reference to all the others. Only after this analysis can the process of conceptual synthesis begin, a process in which the whole is built up again, starting from the most abstract and simple concepts—in this case, value, labor, and so on. Thus the scientific researcher into economics starts with the chaotic apprehension of bourgeois society, analyzes it conceptually by empirical study into its most abstract constituent elements, and then proceeds to synthesize these elements through a dialectical exposition to yield a total conceptual comprehension of the object under study. In essence, this is Hegel's method with the proviso that in Hegel the place of the correct method of analysis and synthesis is taken by the Idea conceived of as an autonomous subject. Hegel had grasped the necessity of moving from the abstract to the concrete but had at the same time mystified his approach by starting with the Idea instead of the empirical content. This is what Marx meant by the famous phrase about having found Hegel standing on his head and put him back on his feet. "My relationship to Hegel is very simple," Marx wrote. "I am a disciple of Hegel and the presumptuous chattering of the epigoni who believe they have buried this eminent thinker seems to me frankly to be ridiculous. However that may be, I have taken the liberty of adopting a critical attitude toward my master, to rid his dialectic of its mysticism and thus to subject it to a profound change."

But though Marx's methodology may have been Hegelian, the concepts with which he was operating were part of a longer tradition—that of the classical economists, in particular Smith and Ricardo. It was this combination that led Lassalle to describe Marx as a "Hegel turned economist and a Ricardo turned socialist." In a sense, Marx was the last and the greatest of the classical economists, for the concepts he used were part of the language common to all economists in the mid-nineteenth century but thereafter abandoned by the orthodox schools of economics. Since the third quarter of the nineteenth century, economists in Western Europe and America have tended to look at the capitalist system as given, to construct models of it assuming private property, profit, and a more-or-less free market, and to discuss the functionings of this model, concentrating particularly on prices. This "marginalist" school of economics has no concept of value apart from price. To Marx, this procedure seemed superficial: he considered it superficial in a literal sense, in that it was only a description of phenomena lying on the surface of capitalist society without an analysis of the mode of production that gave rise to these phenomena; and he thought this approach took the capitalist system for granted, whereas he wished to analyze "the birth, life, and death of a given social organism and its replacement by another, superior order."

Central to the classical theory had been the labor theory of value, according to which the value of objects was measured by the amount of labor embodied in them. This fitted in well with Marx's general view that socially productive labor was the basic factor in economic life. Marx distinguished between use-value and exchange-value. In former times, use-value had been important and objects were exchanged for each other either directly or through the intermediary of money. But under capitalism, the ultimate aim was to turn commodities into money. And the commodity "whose use-value possesses the peculiar property of being a source of value, whose actual consumption, therefore, is itself an embodiment of labor and, consequently, a creation of value" was "the capacity for labor or labor power."

But this labor theory of value seemed to involve the puzzle that in the exchange of capital and labor the wages of the laborer had a smaller exchange-value than the exchange-value of the object he produced. Marx accounted for this phenomenon of profit by means of his theory of surplus-value, which was characterized by Engels as Marx's most important "discovery" in economics. Marx made a distinction between *constant* capital, which was "that part of capital which is represented by the means of production, by the raw material, auxiliary material, and instruments of labor, and does not, in the process of production, undergo any quantitative alteration of value," and *variable* capital. Of this Marx said: "That part of capital, represented by labor power, does, in the process of production, undergo an alteration of value. It both reproduces the equivalent of its own value, and also produces an excess, a surplus-value, which may itself vary, may be more or less according to the circumstances." (It is important to note that Marx talked here of labor *power*—a refinement he introduced into his theory during the 1850s. For plainly, if the exchange-value of a commodity equaled the amount of labor incorporated in it, the exchange-value of a day's labor must be equal to its product, i.e., the wages of the laborer will be the same as his product.) The essential point was that the capitalist got the worker to work longer than was merely sufficient to embody in his product the value of his labor power. For example, if the value of the labor power of the worker (roughly what it cost to keep him and his family alive and capable of working) was $4 a day and if he could embody $4 of value in the product of his work during four hours: then, if he worked eight hours, the second half of his day would yield surplus-value—in this case another $4. The variation in surplus-value mentioned above was called the rate of surplus-value (or rate of exploitation) around which the struggle between capitalists and workers centered. The capitalists were constantly trying to increase the rate of surplus-value by either extending the hours of labor, or making the labor more intensive or more productive. This production of a surplus was not confined to capitalism, but previously the surplus had simply been appropriated by the possessing class. In capitalism, this appropriation was concealed by the apparently free-market bargain by the capitalists and workers who seemed to be merely exchanging equivalents.

The theory of surplus-value also had implications for the long-term future of capitalism. These were: for the capitalists, that their rate of profit would decrease; for the workers, that their relative standard of living would decline; and for the capitalist system as a whole, that it would be shaken by a series of crises that would culminate in a transition to communism.

The tendency for the rate of profit to decline was due, according to Marx, to changes in what he called the organic composition of capital—the ratio of constant to variable capital. Competition among capitalists and technological progress would increase the amount of capital invested in machines as opposed to that paid out in wages. And since it was only labor that produced a surplus, this meant that profits would fall—always supposing that the rate of surplus-value remained unchanged. Marx realized that the tendency for profits to decline could be offset by raising the rate of surplus-value either by increasing labor's productivity or intensity, or by cheapening the cost of raw materials through colonial expansion. But he considered that these were only short-term palliatives which could not prevent the eventual destruction of the system.

Marx foresaw a relative decline in the workers' standard of living as the proportion of the gross national product accruing to the working class would lessen—although, of course, wages might well rise in real terms. For the competition among capitalists was paralleled by competition among workers who were constantly threatened with replacement from the "industrial reserve army," or mass of unemployed. This tended to prevent real wages from rising very much above subsistence level for any considerable length of time. In *Capital*, Marx paints a grim picture of the fate of the working class:

> Within the capitalist system all methods for raising the social productiveness of labor are brought about at the cost of the individual laborer; all means for the development of production transform themselves into means of domination over, and exploitation of, the producers; they mutilate the laborer into a fragment of a man, degrade him to

the level of an appendage of a machine, destroy
every remnant of charm in his work and turn it
into a hated toil; they estrange from him the intellectual potentialities of the labor-process in the
same proportion as science is incorporated in it as
an independent power; they distort the conditions
under which he works, subject him during the
labor-process to a despotism the more hateful for
its meanness; they transform his life-time into
working-time, and drag his wife and child beneath
the wheels of the Juggernaut of capital.

In other of his writings, however, Marx is less pessimis-
tic about the effects of capitalism on the workers. In
the *Grundrisse*, in particular, he admits the possibility
of a drastic reduction in the working day and almost
says that a greatly increased standard of living for
society as a whole is a precondition for a successful
revolution.

Obviously Marx's views in *Capital* on the tendency of
the rate of profit to fall and the decline in working-class
living standards implied a series of crises ahead for the
capitalist system. Marx never produced a unified theory
of the nature of these crises. It was inherent in the
concept of surplus-value that the workers would produce values that exceeded the reimbursement of their
labor. In *Theories of Surplus Value*, Marx wrote: "The
greatest part of the producers, the workers, can only
consume an equivalent for their product so long as they
produce more than this equivalent—surplus value or
surplus product. They must always be over-producers,
must always produce over and above their needs, in

order to be able to be consumers or buyers within the limits of their needs." This contradiction inevitably engendered an economic crisis in which the equilibrium between sale and purchase was more or less re-established. In *Capital*, Marx explicitly pointed to underconsumption as a cause of crisis: "The last real cause of all crises always remains the poverty and restricted consumption of the masses as compared to the tendency of capitalist production to develop the productive forces in such a way that only the absolute power of consumption of the entire society would be their limit." It was certainly Marx's general view that capitalism was an unstable system which only solved the problems it generated by creating even greater obstacles to its future progress. And the eventual conclusion was described in a famous passage at the end of Volume One of *Capital*:

Along with the constantly diminishing number of the magnates of capital, who usurp and monopolize all advantages of this process of transformation, grows the mass of misery, oppression, slavery, degradation, exploitation; but with this too grows the revolt of the working class, a class always increasing in numbers, and disciplined, united, organized by the very mechanism of the process of capitalist production itself. The monopoly of capital becomes a fetter upon the mode of production, which has sprung up and flourished along with, and under it. Centralization of the means of production and socialization of labor at last reach a point where they become incompatible with their capitalist integument. This integument is burst asunder. The knell of capitalist private property sounds. The expropriators are expropriated.

Just *when* the integument would burst asunder, Marx naturally declined to predict with any precision. Indeed, in such writings as the *Grundrisse* the impression was given that it would take a very long time for capital to exhaust all the possibilities for the extraction of surplus-value from the economy. Marx anticipated, in this connection, an era of automation and a stage in capitalism in which manual labor had been replaced by machines wherever possible—an awesome prospect.

Although Marx looked forward to the inevitable collapse of the capitalist system, he was far from having a totally negative view of it. In his outline of the materialist conception of history, he wrote: "New higher relations of production never appear before the material conditions of their existence have matured in the womb of the old society." Thus communism was implicit in capitalism. Among the achievements of capitalism were an enormous increase in social wealth, the progressive unification of the world under a single economic system, and creating the possibility of an individual "whose relationships and capacities are of a general and universal nature." Marx even conceived of capitalism as being forced to overcome the crucial problem of the division of labor:

Modern industry, on the other hand, through its catastrophes imposes the necessity of recognizing, as a fundamental law of production, variation of work, consequently fitness of the laborer for varied

work, consequently the greatest possible development of his varied aptitudes. It becomes a question of life and death for society to adapt the mode
of production to the normal functioning of this
law. Modern industry, indeed, compels society, under penalty of death, to replace the detail-worker
of today, crippled by lifelong repetition of one and
the same trivial operation, and thus reduced to the
mere fragment of a man, by the fully developed
individual, fit for a variety of labors, ready to face
any change of production, and for whom his different social functions are but so many modes of
giving free scope to his own natural and acquired
powers.

Marx considered, too, that certain of the economic
forms of capitalism prepared the way for communism.
He talked, for example, of share capital, "the most perfect form of capital leading to communism," and referred to the joint stock company as "the transcendence
of the capitalist mode of production within the capitalist
mode of production." There was thus a striking contrast between the increasingly social character of the
capitalist process of production and the antisocial character of capitalist private property—a contrast which
in itself summed up Marx's basic critique of capitalism.

It should be remembered that Marx's economics is
not a unified system. He changed his mind on a number
of points during the 1850s—particulary the substitution
of labor-power for labor and the introduction of surplus-
value which altered his perspective considerably. Thus
there was a difference in approach between the rather

simplistic views of capitalist breakdown in *The Communist Manifesto* and the views expressed in the *Grundrisse*, which took into account the fact that the idea of "subsistence" had a historical element in it, that parts of the working class had become better off, and that there had been a growth in social groups living on the surplus from productive labor. There is also the fact that Marx's work remained unfinished. He was always mentioning in his correspondence new materials that needed to be assimilated before he could interpret them in a scientific synthesis. Whether he was also discouraged by the sheer theoretical difficulties entailed by his own premises is an open question.

What, finally, are we to make of Marx's claim to have founded a "science" of economics? Most importantly, science for Marx was not equated with natural science. (The German term *Wissenschaft* has a much wider connotation than the English word "science.") Throughout his life Marx was clear that natural science would have to lose what he called its "one-sidedly materialist orientation" in order to be integrated in a total interpretation of man and society. Particularly in his later writings, Marx emphasized that any science had to penetrate from the apparent movement of things to their real underlying causes. This involved a distinction between appearance and essence going back a long way from Hegel through Spinoza to Aristotle. Marx was distinctive in conceiving of economics as the core of any scientific view of society and in criticizing, from his early writings onward, the current conception of economics which dealt only with the market system (appearance) without considering the social foundation (essence) on which the market was based. There are two factors which militate against treating Marx's views as scientific in the vulgar sense of theories that can be shown to be true or false by observation. First, there is obviously some sort of continuity between Marx's early and later writings: the notions of alienation, of man as a self-creating being, and of history as a progress leading to an unalienated society are central to all Marx's work. Thus his writings always incorporate a normative element, which means that they are not subject to direct refutation simply by reference to "fact." Second, Marx's economic theories are models, more or less removed from empirical reality, and they merely describe tendencies. Thus the labor theory of value is not something which is right or wrong. For Marx, it is true by definition, and the real question is whether it is able to account for the movement of prices and profits. This is a very complex question. For example, it was Marx's view that, in general, commodities tended to exchange at prices which were proportionate to the value embodied in them—although there might be temporary variations. In Volume Three of *Capital* Marx changed his view somewhat by admitting that what determined the exchange of commodities was much more their cost of production. And the exact relationship of values to prices has been a constant source of debate ever since. Again, central to Marx's view of the fate of capitalism was the doctrine of the falling rate of profit. Yet it is extremely difficult to determine the validity of this doctrine. In the United States, for example, profits seem on the whole not to have fallen over the last century or so—in spite of the fact that constant capital has grown much faster than the labor force. But, of course, the productivity per worker has also vastly increased and so there is no reason why profits should have declined. The most that can be said is that it is very difficult to determine the status of theories that involve so many variables.

Whatever importance he ascribed to the long-term determining effect of the economy, and however much time he devoted to analyzing its present and future course, Marx was always more than an economist. He was always concerned to link his economic studies— the "objective" side of his dialectic—with its "subjective" side, involving the concepts of class, party, and revolution through which men became politically conscious of the tensions in the capitalist economy and "shortened the birth-pangs" of communism

POLITICS

The central institution of capitalist society and the main target of Marx's politics was the State. In his early writings Marx had been concerned to emphasize the gap between civil society and the State viewed as the projection of the alienated essence of man. Later, he evolved a different (though not incompatible) view of the State as an instrument of class domination. This view is most clearly expressed in *The Communist Manifesto*: "Political power, properly so called, is merely the organized power of one class for oppressing another. . . . The executive of the modern state is but a committee

for managing the affairs of the whole bourgeoisie."
Marx traced the origin of the State, together with other
social institutions and classes, to the division of labor:
the State was opposed to the real interests of all members of society because it constituted an illusory sense
of community serving as a screen for the real struggles
waged by classes against each other. In the course of
history each method of production gave rise to a typical
political organization furthering the interests of the
dominant class. The large-scale industry and universal
competition of modern capitalism had created their own
political organization—the modern liberal democratic
state under which the bourgeoisie could best develop its
class potential.

It has already been noted that Marx's materialist conception of history was a very flexible tool of analysis—
and his view of the State was no exception. Marx once
said that the only perfect example of the State as an instrument of class domination was North America. For
the political sphere was not merely the plaything of economic undercurrents. Sometimes, Marx said, the same
economic system could give rise to different political
systems. Indeed, in certain circumstances, politics could
dominate economics: it was the Tudor governments, for
example, that created the conditions for the existence of
British capitalism; and Marx always recognized that,
although England was more advanced than France
economically, the political consciousness of the French
was superior to that of the English.

Marx admitted two general exceptions to his characterization of the State as an instrument of class

domination. The first he did not go into with any great detail: in the Asian societies of India, China, and, to some extent, Russia, Marx saw a despotism which, being mainly based on the absence of private property in land, did not serve the interests of a particular class. The second exception was more important: Marx believed that in a situation where two or more contending classes were of more or less equal strength, the State could attain a large degree of independence and become a virtual parasite on the whole of society. This particularly applied to the period of absolute monarchy following the decline of feudalism. "Modern historical research," he wrote, "has shown how modern absolute monarchy appeared in the period of transition when the old feudal classes were decaying and the medieval burgher class was evolving into the modern bourgeois class, without either of the disputing parties being able to settle accounts with the other." And he found a more contemporary example in the French Second Empire under Napoleon III.

On whatever base it was constituted, the State was, for Marx, central to the alienating structure of capitalist society, and only a revolution could displace its pervasive influence. Because the existence of the State was bound up with the existence of classes, the State could not be abolished piecemeal. All previous revolutions had simply replaced one form of State by another more suited to the changing mode of production. And the form of State that went along with capitalism—liberal democracy—was no exception. Although liberal democracy held that it was open to everyone to emancipate himself by becoming a bourgeois, by definition not everyone could do so and the inevitable result was the exploitation of one group in society by another. However, the most important characteristic of the next revolution—the proletarian one—was that it would be social and not merely political: it would not proclaim abstract rights that only a few could enjoy, but achieve a general emancipation by penetrating to the real life of man—his socioeconomic life.

Marx was no prophet, and he did not go in for detailed predictions about the future revolution. But he did say something about when he thought a revolution might occur, where it would break out, whether it would be violent or not, and who would carry it out.

WHEN? Marx was always scathing about those he referred to as "the alchemists of revolution" who tried to provoke revolt whatever the socioeconomic circumstances. Not surprisingly, however, his optimism about the imminence of the revolution was strongest during the two periods when he was actively engaged in politics: the upheavals of 1848 and the First International. In *The Communist Manifesto* he declared, "the bourgeois revolution in Germany will be but the prelude to an immediately following proletarian revolution." He maintained this view even after the failure of the revolutionary movement, and it was not until he resumed his economic studies in London in 1850 that he realized that "a new revolution is possible only in consequence of a new crisis," and told the workers that "you have to endure and go through fifteen, twenty, fifty years of civil war in order to change the circum-

stances, in order to make yourselves fit for power."
Marx's revolutionary optimism had a brief renaissance
during and immediately after the Paris Commune, when
he conceived of the possibility of a successful proletarian
revolution in countries where the majority of the population were peasants. But his mature economic writings
took a more long-term view of the economic causes of
revolution and in the *Grundrisse* the impression was
given that capitalism had a very long way to go before
it exhausted its capacities to exploit the enormous possibilities created by machinery.

WHERE? The simple view of class polarization and
impoverishment contained in *The Communist Manifesto* seemed to imply that a proletarian revolution was
uniquely a consequence of industrialization. However,
between 1848 and the founding of the First International, Marx's views underwent an important change in
this respect: he came to believe that workers could hope
for substantial gains within the capitalist state—hence
the importance he attributed to the Ten Hours' Act; and
he realized that considerable differentiation within the
industrial working class occurred with the emergence
of a labor aristocracy. He also came to see that potential
European revolutions would be more and more con-
tingent on the general world situation. In 1859 he referred to the opening up of California, Australia, and
the Far East and continued: "Revolution is imminent on
the Continent and also will immediately assume a
socialist character. Can it avoid being crushed in this
small corner, because bourgeois society is in the ascend-
ant over much larger areas of the earth?" Later still,

Marx began to think that Russia might prove the starting point of the revolution which "begins this time in
the East, hitherto the invulnerable bulwark and rein-
forcement of the counterrevolution." And a year before
his death he wrote: "If the Russian revolution becomes
the signal for a proletarian revolution in the West, so
that both complete each other, then the present Russian
system of community ownership of land could serve as
the starting point for a communist development." As his
hopes of Russia rose, so those of Britain declined. He
considered in general that the English lacked "the spirit
of generalization and revolutionary fervor." Moreover,
the British proletariat as a whole had done too well out
of their world economic dominance and the labor aristocracy had improved their relative standard of living
too much not to dampen down their revolutionary im-
petus.

How? Marx did not believe in the inevitability of
violent revolution. In some of the most advanced countries he considered that revolution could be introduced
by peaceful means. In 1872 he mentioned Great Britain,
the United States, and possibly Holland in this context;
and in 1880 he wrote:

> My party considers an English revolution not *neces-
> sary*, but—according to historic precedents—*pos-
> sible*. If the unavoidable evolution turn into a rev-
> olution, it would not only be the fault of the ruling
> classes, but also of the working class. Every pacific
> concession of the former has been wrung from
> them by "pressure from without." Their action kept
> pace with that pressure and if the latter has more

and more weakened, it is only because the English
working class know not how to wield their power
and use their liberties, both of which they possess
legally.

But Marx did not turn into a tame parliamentarian in
his old age. He was vigorous in condemning the Commune for observing too many legal niceties in a crisis
situation, and not being willing to start a civil war. He
declared to a conference of the International in 1871:
"We must make clear to the governments: we know that
you are the armed power that is directed against the
proletariat; we will proceed against you by peaceful
means where that is possible and with arms when it is
necessary." But however much Marx thought that sometimes force could be the midwife of revolution, he never
(except briefly in 1848 and under Tsarist conditions in
Russia) approved of the use of revolutionary terror. He
strongly criticized the Jacobins' use of terror in the
French Revolution; its use was for him a sign of the
weakness and immaturity of that revolution, which had
to impose by violence what was not yet inherent in
society. Any revolution, if the socioeconomic circumstances were not appropriate, inevitably led to a reign
of terror during which the revolutionary powers attempted to reorganize society from above. Finally, Marx
considered that a successful revolution—at least in the
long run—was impossible if confined to one country.
Marx criticized the leaders of the French proletariat in
1848 for thinking that "they would be able to consum-
mate a proletarian revolution within the national walls
of France, side by side with the remaining bourgeois

nations." But, equally, Marx considered a strong national unity to be essential for the degree of working-class organization to produce a revolution and was strongly in favor of the unification of Germany and Italy and the resurgence of Polish nationalism.

WHO? Although Marx believed that a political party was necessary to carry out a successful revolution, he never founded a party. He was a member of any party organization for only a few years and always based his political activities on existing working-class organizations. Of course, the concept of a political party in a modern sense is consequent on mass democracy and was only developing very gradually during Marx's lifetime. In *The Communist Manifesto*, Marx outlined the three defining characteristics of the Communist party as follows: "1. In the national struggles of the proletarians of the different countries they point out and bring to the front the common interests of the entire proletariat, independent of all nationality. 2. In the various stages of development which the struggle of the working class against the bourgeoisie has to pass through, they always and everywhere represent the interests of the movement as a whole. . . . 3. Theoretically, they have over the great mass of the proletariat the advantage of clearly understanding the line of march, the conditions and the ultimate general results of the proletarian movement." But even the Communist League (in which Marx was active from 1847 to 1852) was never a political party in this sense: it had only about 300 members and was forced to operate in a semiclandestine manner. Indeed, it was temporarily dissolved by Marx in 1848, and it was only in the last months of the revolution that he realized the need for a separate organized workers' party. The First International, on the other hand, was in no way a Communist party, nor did Marx's followers form a separate group inside it. On the whole, Marx was in favor of open, democratic organization, with decisions taken by majority votes at national conferences; and he was always more willing to look for areas of agreement than of difference. Thus Marx's concept of the party was never some ideal institution, but was always based on the level of organization and consciousness already in existence. Nevertheless, he did insist that this party should have a completely democratic internal organization; that it should be the independent creation of the workers themselves; that it should be distinguished by a theoretical understanding of working-class goals; and that (usually) its organization was not to be a part of, or dependent on, any other political party.

There has been much debate about the kind of society a proletarian revolution would inaugurate and some criticism of the vagueness of Marx's sketches of it. But it is essential to remember that—on Marx's own principles—any detailed predictions were bound to be baseless. For all ideas were rooted in the socioeconomic soil of their time, and descriptions of the future would thus be rootless ideas without any foundation in reality. Marx would have agreed completely with Hegel that "it is just as silly to suppose that any philosophy goes beyond its contemporary world, as that an individual can jump beyond his time." Yet it is plain that for Marx the most fundamental achievement of a proletarian revolution would be (in broad terms) the changed relationship of man to nature and to his fellow men—and, in consequence, the disappearance of political oppression in the form of the State.

For the materialist conception of history, the organization of man's productive forces was fundamental, and the proletarian revolution would be the first revolution to introduce a nonantagonistic mode of production. There would be no more occasion for the exploitation of the majority by the minority, since the means of production would be in the hands of the working class and the wealth of society would be used for the benefit of society as a whole. In particular the division of labor (which Marx believed to be at the root of so many social evils) would be abolished. In a well-known passage in *The German Ideology*, Marx stated:

In communist society, where nobody has one exclusive sphere of activity but each can become accomplished in any branch he wishes, society regulates the general production and thus makes it possible for me to do one thing today and another tomorrow, to hunt in the morning, fish in the afternoon, rear cattle in the evening, criticize after dinner, whatever I have a mind, without ever becoming hunter, fisherman, shepherd, or critic. This fixation of social activity, this consolidation of what we ourselves produce into an objective power above us, growing out of our control, thwarting our expectations, bringing to naught our calculations, is one of the chief factors in historical development up till now.

Of course, there are obvious difficulties in applying this essentially rural description to a highly developed society. In the *Grundrisse*, Marx implied that the whole problem of the division of labor would be bypassed by the introduction of automated machinery and the drastic reduction in the working day: the problem then would no longer be labor but how to use leisure time. But as he grew older, he grew less sanguine: at the very end of *Capital*, Volume Three, he admitted that however much labor could be humanized under socialism, "it nevertheless still remains a realm of necessity. Beyond it begins that development of human energy which is an end in itself, the true realm of freedom, which, however, can only blossom forth with this realm of necessity as its basis. The shortening of the working day is its basic prerequisite."

The resolution of problems such as the exact distribution of the social product, the role of money, and the future of marriage and the family would ultimately be dependent on the modification of human drives by changing the socioeconomic basis of society. Here Marx distinguished between constant desires, "which exist under all circumstances, only their form and direction being changed by different social circumstances," and relative desires, "which owe their origin merely to a particular form of society, to particular conditions of production and exchange." In a communist society, the former would merely be changed and given the opportunity to develop normally, whereas the latter would be destroyed by being deprived of the conditions of their existence. Marx continued: "Which desires would be merely altered under a communist organization and which would be dissolved, can only be decided in a practical way, through the changing of real, practical desires, and not through historical comparisons with earlier historical circumstances." He went on to mention several desires (among them the desire to eat) as examples of fixed desires, and continued: "neither do the communists envisage abolishing the fixity of desires and needs . . . they only aim to organize production and exchange in such a way as to make possible the normal satisfaction of all desires, that is, a satisfaction limited only by the desires themselves."

The political corollary of the abolition of the division of labor in communist society was the disappearance of the State. Marx stated forthrightly: "As soon as the goal of the proletarian movement, the abolition of classes, shall have been reached, the power of the State, whose function is to keep the great majority of producers beneath the yoke of a small minority of exploiters, will disappear and governmental functions will be transformed into simple administrative functions." What this meant in concrete terms was that communism would no longer need the typical components of the State—bureaucracy, a standing army, and a professional judicature. Marx's most revealing comments in this connection are his remarks on the Paris Commune. Although Marx did not approve of all the Commune's policies, he welcomed the Commune's proposals to have all officials, including judges, elected by universal suffrage and their tenure to be revocable at any time; to pay officials the same wages as workmen; to replace the standing army by the armed people; and to divest the police and clergy of their political influence. Marx also believed that, given time, the initiative of the Commune could have given rise, in the country as a whole, to a decentralized, federal political structure and an economy based on co-operatives united by a common plan.

Marx was clear, of course, that a situation in which "the normal satisfaction of all desires" was possible could not be arrived at immediately. After a successful proletarian revolution there would be a period of transition which he occasionally referred to as "the dictatorship of the proletariat." (It should be noted that the word "dictatorship" did not have the same connotation for Marx as it does nowadays. He associated it principally with the Roman office of *dictatura*, where all power was legally concentrated in the hands of a single man during a limited period in a time of crisis.) Even with the abolition of the division of labor and the consequent disappearance of the State, communist society would still "in every respect, economically, morally, and intellectually, be stamped with the birthmarks of the old society from whose womb it emerges." Only after a considerable period could full communism be attained. This communism Marx described in a famous passage that can serve as an apt summary of his ultimate goal:

In a higher phase of communist society, after the enslaving subordination of the individual to the division of labor, and therewith also the antithesis between mental and physical labor, has vanished; after labor has become not only a means of life but life's prime want; after the productive forces have also increased with the all-round development of the individual, and all the springs of co-operative wealth flow more abundantly—only then can the narrow horizon of bourgeois right be crossed in its entirety and society inscribe on its banners: From each according to his ability, to each according to his need!

The Reputation

iii

The aim of this concluding chapter is to give a historical sketch of the different interpretations to which Marx's thought has been subject. This is necessary for an understanding of Marx because his ideas have been overlaid by a series of reinterpretations, some of which are highly misleading. However impossible it may be to uncover some essentially "real" Marx, an appreciation of Marx's ideas is easier once these interpretations have been placed in historical and political perspective.

Three main reasons can be distinguished for the capacity of Marx to seem all things to all men. Firstly, many of his doctrines really *were* ambiguous. In his youth, Marx had detected an ambivalence in his master Hegel, and the same ambivalence was present—not surprisingly—in the disciple. For each was a dialectical thinker, and the Marxian dialectic in particular was open-ended: being a unity of subjective and objective factors, both the theory and the practice were constantly interacting and evolving. Marx had not offered any hard-and-fast conclusions—only a methodology. This ambivalence was heightened by the fact that Marx's work was unfinished: of his vast projected "Economics" only the first volume of the first part—Volume One of *Capital*—was ever published in his lifetime. In addition, Marx's power for sustained creative work deserted him during the last illness-ridden decade of his life, and he was not able to contribute to the debate that began after the Paris Commune and the publication of *Capital*; it was only in the 1880s that his doctrines gained widespread attention. Marx's view on some of the subsequent applications of his theory can be gauged from his comment on certain French "Marxists": "As for me, I am *not* a Marxist!"

The second reason for the changing nature of what came to be known as Marxism was its becoming the doctrine of a mass movement. Mass political parties were born in the second half of the nineteenth century and socialism was the most radical, appealing to all who were excluded from, or not getting enough of, the benefits of the new industrial society. What distinguished Marxism in this context was its rare ability to link revolutionary fervor and desire for change with a historical perspective and a claim to be scientific. Almost inevitably, the ideas were simplified, rigidified, ossified. Marxism became a matter of simple faith for its millions of adherents to whom it gave the certainty of final victory. But this entailed its transformation into a dogmatic ideology with the correlative concept of heresy —or revisionism, as it was often called. (The parallels with certain periods in the history of the Christian religion are obvious.) Only a very selective version of the sacred texts could be propagated, and if even then history did not conform—then history itself had to be rewritten.

The third factor was the chaotic state in which Marx left his manuscripts at his death. Not only was his work unfinished, but the rough drafts that went beyond what he had actually published implied—at least in the minds of many—a thorough reassessment of his message. The publication of Marx's early writings around 1930 and the *Grundrisse* in 1941 are the most striking examples (see below, p. 86).

It is an important fact (given excessive prominence in the orthodox Communist interpretation of Marx) that Marx had had a lifelong friend and collaborator in Friedrich Engels. Engels gave Marx constant moral and financial support, and he had a considerable influence on Marx's thought. It was Engels, in 1844, who guided Marx's interest to economics and introduced him at first hand to British capitalism; Marx relied on him, too, for advice on military and scientific matters. But the fact that Engels survived Marx by thirteen years enabled him to have an even greater effect on the interpretation of Marx's thought just as it was beginning to become the official doctrine of a mass political movement. Engels was the keeper of Marx's archives and the authoritative exponent of Marx's ideas—beginning with his editing Marx's manuscripts of the remaining volumes of *Capital*. He was a quick and lucid writer, a vulgarizer in the best sense possible, and the systematization and clarity of his works gave them a much wider circulation than any of Marx's writings. Engels's contribution was to assimilate Marx's views more and more to the prevailing positivism and scientism—a process begun with his speech at Marx's graveside: "Just as Darwin discovered the law of development of organic nature, so Marx discovered the law of development of human history." This assimilation received its most popular exposition in *Anti-Dühring*, which for decades after Marx's death continued to be accepted as the classical account of the Marxist *Weltanschauung*. In his attack on the socialist philosopher Dühring, Engels proclaimed the Marxian dialectic to be "the science of the general laws of motion and development of nature, human society, and thought." More specifically, the most important of these were the laws of the transformation of quantity into quality, of the interpretation of opposites, and of the negation of the negation. (Of course, Marx also called his doctrines "scientific" [see above, p. 60], but the term had much less the connotation of natural-scientific methodology in his work—after all, even Hegel had called his work "scientific.") Engels thought these laws to be operative in a nature that was objectively given and independent of the human mind. Thus the world of nature and the world of human history were two separate fields of study—whereas for Marx one of the central aspects of his dialectic had consisted precisely in the interaction of man and his surroundings, a view stemming from Hegel. Engels did indeed claim to be simply applying Hegel's dialectic, and, in a sense, Hegel also saw a dialectic in nature but it was still subject to the universal mediation of human consciousness. The concept of matter as some kind of *materia prima* is entirely foreign to Marx (see above, p. 37).

During the two decades after Engels's death Marx's ideas came to dominate the socialist movement in Western Europe and in particular its largest and best-organized party, the German Social Democratic Party. For the orthodox Marxists of the SPD, led by Karl Kautsky, Marx was primarily a great economist who had demonstrated with scientific rigor the inevitable collapse of capitalism and the victory of the proletariat. This view was already under attack by the revisionist school. Their chief protagonist was Edward Bernstein, who had been much influenced by the Fabian socialism he had met in England. Bernstein considered himself a Marxist but thought that Marx needed revising to fit his ideas to the world of modern industrial democracy. He denied that classes were polarizing and their struggle sharpening, and he advocated a socialism that would be introduced peacefully by reform rather than revolution. This view was sharply contested by Kautsky who, as the champion of Marx's ideas against heresy, carried further and into new fields the systematization begun by Engels. He emphasized the aspects of Marx's work which laid stress on the determination of history by economic causes and preached a value-free, scientific Marxism in which history was governed by immutable laws. In the revisionist controversy, Kautsky could plausibly claim to be the upholder of orthodoxy; but it should be remembered that Marx's ideas were chiefly known through the stark proclamations of *The Communist Manifesto* or the difficult volumes of *Capital*: less than half of what Marx had written—including work that was to throw a different light on many of those debates— had so far been published. Kautsky and the leaders of the loose federation of Marxist parties known as the Second International most evidently departed from Marx's ideas in the ever-growing gulf between their theory and their practice. For however much they might protest their orthodoxy in such matters as the class struggle and the inevitability of socialism, their practice had to be adapted to the needs of an established party with an increasingly bureaucratic structure operating in a democracy. Inevitably it was more concerned with pulling in votes and conserving its established status and organization than with promoting revolutionary efforts that ran the risk of destroying all its hard-won achievements—an ambiguous situation much like that in which the French and Italian Communist parties currently find themselves.

The German Social Democrat current of Marxism was shattered by the outbreak of World War I. Having become so involved in the political structure of their country, party members found it impossible to resist the tide of patriotic fervor and voted for war credits. The abortive revolution of 1918 and the rise of fascism meant the eclipse of Marxism in Germany for many decades. The center of revolutionary dynamism moved eastward—as toward the end of his life Marx had begun to suspect it might. The Marxism that eventually triumphed in Russia owed a great deal to indigenous elements. In the famous dispute between Mensheviks and Bolsheviks, two of the main issues were whether Russia was on the eve of a bourgeois revolution with the proletarian one a long way off and how centralized the revolutionary party should be. These were both problems that bothered Marx during the 1848 upheavals—not surprisingly, for that was the period when German conditions most resembled the semifeudal, semicapitalist Russia of the first two decades of this century. Marx's writings of this period could provide some support for Lenin's curious idea of a proletariat leading a "bourgeois" revolution, his positive attitude to the peasantry as an essential component of the revolution, and even the idea of permanent revolution that Lenin adopted from Trotsky in April 1917. On the whole, however, the Mensheviks' idea that the revolution could not be hastened and their distrust of a highly centralized party structure were more in accord with Marx's general views. Thus it is not surprising that the Bolsheviks put more emphasis on the political side of Marx's writings than did the German Social Democrats: it is recorded that Lenin knew Marx's circulars to the Communist League "by heart" and "used to delight in quoting them." But the Leninist theory of the party went far beyond anything that Marx had suggested. Lenin believed that the working class could not by itself achieve a revolutionary consciousness; this needed to be instilled in them by a "vanguard" party. He, therefore, wished to see the whole working-class movement subject to a small, highly disciplined and highly centralized party of professional revolutionaries most of whom would be classless intellectuals.

After the success of the 1917 Revolution the ever-growing power of Stalin entailed the formulation of Communist doctrine as a state ideology as far removed from Marx as were the decisions of the Council of Trent from the New Testament. Marx himself had had something to say about a premature revolution having to resort to terror to maintain itself in power, and the idea of a vanguard party soon led to the proletariat's finding itself expropriated by an increasingly dictatorial party machine and eventually by a single man. The monolithic view of the world as subject to dialectical laws, prominent in Engels's *Anti-Dühring* and which Lenin continued, reached its apogee in the Stalinist textbooks on dialectical materialism—a phrase first used by Lenin's mentor Plekhanov. The working class was merely the passive recipient, whether of doctrines or of five-year plans worked out "above." The one major innovation of Stalin in Marxist doctrine, and the main source of his quarrel with Trotsky, was the idea of "socialism in one country"—a view with which Marx would have been distinctly out of sympathy.

In the face of such a rigidification of Marxist theory, a reaction was inevitable. The diminishing vitality of Marxism as a theory went hand in hand with a decreasing interest in the Hegelian elements present in Marx, culminating during the Stalinist period with the condemnation of Hegel as a reactionary thinker pure and simple. It is significant that Lenin himself, just before the 1917 Revolution, had begun to appreciate the significance of Hegel for Marx. But it was George Lukács who rediscovered in full Marx's debt to Hegel and expounded Marx's whole thought, including his economics, within the framework of a social humanism. He restored to the interpretation of Marx the centrality of the notion of alienation—a concept that had been almost entirely absent from Engels onward. Lukács, in his seminal *History and Class Consciousness* (1923), reintroduced the vision of alienated man transcending his alienation through proletarian class consciousness and revolution. As a Hegelian, Lukács rejected the tendency of previous decades to reduce Marxism to a factual science. To suppose that existing social arrangements were governed by the kind of immutable laws operative in physical science was, for Lukács, to suffer an illusion. In this illusion social reality took on the "objective" appearance of something external and independent of man, "reified" as Lukács called it, instead of being seen as the creation of man. Social facts could only be given meaning by understanding the structure of the totality. This totality was dynamic and the highest point it reached was in the class consciousness of the proletariat (viewed as an "ideal type" of Lukács's teacher Weber) which provided the vantage point for viewing current social reality. And in the ultimate analysis this higher class consciousness was identical with Marxism itself. It is a startling fact that Lukács's interpretation of Marx was written *before* the publication of Marx's early writings which contained much which supported his views. Nevertheless, Lukács's ideas did not get wide publicity at the time, although writers like Karl Korsch and Antonio Gramsci stressed the need for Marxists to engage in intellectual debate and criticized the mechanistic themes of the Marxism of the Second International.

For many interpreters of Marx's thought, the publication of the early writings around 1930 marked a decisive turning point. (The impact came later in the English-speaking world—the first translation of the EPM was not published until 1959.) These writings—and particularly the EPM—revealed a Marx very different from either the rather arid economist of Kautsky or the dialectical materialist of Soviet dogma. Marx appeared to be a philosopher, a humanist with not only a devastating account of the alienation of man in capitalist society but also a rich and varied account of the potential latent in every individual waiting to be realized under communism. The subsequent enthusiasm for the early Marx was helped by two factors. First, there had been a revival of interest in Hegel, of which the work of Lukács was but one symptom, and since the early writings of Marx most directly showed the influence of Hegel, the ground was well prepared. Second, leading Marxist theoreticians had previously been at pains to claim that their *Weltanschauung* was totally different from that of the bourgeoisie, but to combat the menace of fascism, Marxists in general were more willing to admit the similarities between Marx's humanism and the humanism of the liberal bourgeoisie

as against the barbarities of Nazi and Fascist ideology
viewed as a rejection of the West European tradition.

The stifling of intellectual life in Germany during the
1930s and World War II meant that—at least in the
Western world—serious attention was paid to Marx's
early writings only in the late 1940s. The widespread
enthusiasm for existentialist doctrines at this time in-
sured a welcome reception for the "young" Marx. Typical
was the wide-selling book by Erich Fromm, *Marx's Concept of Man*, in which Marx was hailed as a spiritualist
existentialist and comparisons were made between
Marxism and Zen Buddhism. Christian-Marxist dialogue
became common: after all, both Kierkegaard and Marx
could be viewed as sharing an existential revolt against
Hegel. In the calm and prosperous 1950s it was difficult
sometimes to believe in the increasing pauperization of
the proletariat and the necessity of its coming to a
realization of its revolutionary role. The growing manip-
ulative power and anonymity of technology, on the
other hand, caused many radicals to take up Marx's
account of the alienation of man in capitalist society and
claim that, in this connection, Marx's views were more
relevant the more wealthy and complex society became.
The subjective factor in man's picture of his world was
being increasingly emphasized, whether in psycho-
analysis or with the stress in linguistics on the active
role of language in shaping human knowledge. And
Marx, too, came to be acceptable to many as a thinker
aiding man's self-comprehension by means, for example,
of his doctrine of ideology.

In Eastern Europe, where Marxism, instead of being the creed of the underdog, had been enthroned as the ruling ideology, there was obviously room to point out that the communist man of the EPM did not have much to do with state bureaucracies of the Stalinist type, and the cautious thesis was advanced, by writers such as Adam Schaff, that alienation could exist even under socialism. Study of the early writings was seen by many anti-Stalinist Marxists as a return to the original source of communist thought, much as the Reformers used the New Testament to show up abuses rife in the later medieval Church. Up to the present time this process has had little effect: Ernst Bloch and Leszek Kolakowski have left their countries, Roger Garaudy has been expelled from the French Communist Party, and the Praxis group of Yugoslavian philosophers is increasingly isolated.

With the publication of Marx's early works, the interpretation of his thought came increasingly to concentrate on the question of its continuity: were there two Marxes—an early and a late, or only one? The old Stalinist interpretation dismissed the early writings as so many *juvenilia* rendered quite superfluous by his later works. And others who wished to minimize the importance of the early writings stressed the infrequency with which Marx later used terms such as "species-being" and "alienation" that were so central to the EPM. Quite the contrary view was taken by the first editors of the German edition of the rediscovered writings. For them, the EPM was "the cardinal point of Marx's whole life's work" which "sets out in its complex web of philosophical, economic, and historical discussions the unity and totality of Marx's intellectual contribution." The even later publication of the *Grundrisse* showed both extreme positions to be mistaken, but the precise nature of the "continuity" is still the subject of much controversy.

In recent years in the Western world two main currents of Marxian interpretation have achieved prominence. The first is that of the Frankfurt School of "critical" theorists such as Adorno, Habermas, and Marcuse. The critical theorists aim to restore the philosophical dimension to Marxism and, retaining an enviable confidence in the power of human rationality, have developed a series of concepts intended to go beyond Marx to interpret the changes that have taken place in the world since his death. These consist mainly in adding the dimension of social psychology to Marx's work and emphasizing the basic proposition that if society is increasingly under the artificial control of technocrats then any purely empirical approach to social reality must end up as a defense of that control. The most striking statement in this context is Jurgen Habermas's *Knowledge and Human Interests*. The influence of Freud—so manifestly absent from previous Marxist writing—has been felt by all the Frankfurt School but in particular by Herbert Marcuse whose *Eros and Civilization* attempted a synthesis of Freud and Marx. But it was *One Dimensional Man* which made Marcuse famous, particularly when some of its ideas seemed to offer an interpretation of the student revolts of the late 1960s. Marcuse's pessimism about the revolutionary potential of a proletariat dominated (along with the rest of society)

by an all-pervasive technocratic ideology led him to place
his faith in the substratum of the outcast and outsiders,
the exploited and persecuted minorities such as students
and blacks which would involve a meeting of "the most
advanced consciousness of humanity and its most exploited force." Obviously, there is no direct parallel in
Marx to the students, and the appeal to a force *outside*
society is more reminiscent of the anarchists than of
Marx, whose views on the *Lumpenproletariat* were the
exact opposite.

The second current interpretation—the school of
Louis Althusser—is worth spending a little more time
on because it represents itself as a direct interpretation
of Marx. Taking advantage of the current prestige of
structuralist linguistics, psychology, and anthropology,
it is the aim of Althusser to "rehabilitate" Marx as a
structuralist before his time. Thus Althusser continues
the Stalinist division of an early pre-Marxist Marx and
a later scientific Marx—though with a conceptual so-
phistication quite foreign to the previous versions of
this view. Roughly speaking, structuralism is the view
that the key to the understanding of a social system is
the structural relationship of its parts—the way these
parts are related together by the regulative principle of
the system. And Althusser's search for a timeless rationality reminiscent of Comte (for whom Marx himself
had no time) involves the banishment of both history
and philosophy. When applied to Marx, this involves
cutting his work into two separate conceptual structures
with the dividing point around 1845. Any reading of
Marx as a humanist, a Hegelian, or a historicist must

(since these ideas are clearly contained in his early works) be rejected. Since it has become increasingly implausible to claim (particularly after the publication of the *Grundrisse*) that there are no humanist or Hegelian elements in the later Marx, a "real" Marx has been uncovered employing a methodology—never clearly defined—almost totally at variance with concepts that he actually employs.

In spite of their being so clearly at variance in many places with what Marx actually *said*, the ideas of Althusser have had considerable success. For Althusser's Marx is clearly incompatible with existentialism and radical versions of Christianity and thus attractive to those who felt that their commitment was becoming diluted by "dialogue." Its esoteric emphasis on theoretical analysis and its disdain for empirical work are also welcome to intellectuals. Obviously anyone is entitled to revise Marx—but it is disingenuous to claim that such revisions really represent a return to Marx.

Finally, what of the paradox that Marx, a Victorian thinker who saw Europe and North America as the center of the world stage and the arena for future revolutions, is apparently now more widely respected as a mentor by the populations of Third World countries? Marx himself certainly emphasized the European limitations of his theory of historical development. He talked of the Asiatic mode of production, but he did not integrate it into his scheme of historical development. According to him, this mode of production was static and destined to be overtaken by the spread of capitalism over the whole globe. Thus Marx was as ambivalent on colonialism as he was on capitalism—both were destructive and inhuman but at the same time regenerative in that they laid the foundations for a new form of society. This emerges particularly from Marx's analysis of the British in India. There is little in African socialism or Chinese communism that represents a distinct interpretation of Marx himself. It is most important to bear in mind in this connection that Marx envisaged a communist revolution taking place in countries where a certain degree of economic well-being would permit considerable postrevolutionary political freedom. In the event, however, Marxist doctrines have proved most successful in those countries where scarcity of resources mean that political freedom is a luxury they cannot affcrd. In many developing countries a version of Marxism combined with nationalism functions as an ideology for mass participation in the modernization process. The central doctrine of Maoism—the "mass line" and the encirclement of the towns by the countryside which spring mainly from the experience of extended guerrilla warfare—is far removed from the original ideas of Marx, though obviously in the broad scheme of Marxism the people of Asia, Africa, and Latin America can be substituted as an "external proletariat" in the place of the industrial working class in which Marx placed such hope, and the theory of imperialism can take the place of Marx's exploitation.

The ideas of Marx—revised, distorted, rediscovered—have been the inspiration of a large section of humanity over the last hundred years. The history of their influence has shown the validity of the conclusion of

Ignazio Silone with which, I think, Marx himself would not have disagreed:

"The more Socialist theories claim to be 'scientific,' the more transitory they are; but Socialist values are permanent. The distinction between theories and values is not sufficiently recognized, but it is fundamental. On a group of theories one can found a school; but on a group of values one can found a culture, a civilization, a new way of living together among men."

HOW TO READ MARX:
A SHORT BIBLIOGRAPHY

INDEX

HOW TO READ MARX:
A SHORT BIBLIOGRAPHY

Anyone setting out to read Marx in English is faced with a problem: there is an embarrassingly large collection of selected writings of one sort and another, but no complete works as yet. The latter started publication, in New York and London, early in 1975 and will be appearing regularly over the next dozen years or so—finally to total a daunting fifty volumes. Meanwhile, the Foreign Languages Publishing House in Moscow has produced separate editions of many of Marx's works. Although the introductions and notes are often written from an extremely committed point of view, the translations themselves are quite faithful.

Undoubtedly the best short piece of Marx to read is *The Communist Manifesto*. Although Marx realized it needed updating (see the Preface to the second German edition) he was continually willing for it to be re-edited and translated as a summary of his views. There is a cheap Penguin edition (though the long introduction is unfairly hostile to Marx) and even cheaper editions from Moscow and Peking.

The next work to read is the first part of *The German Ideology* (the last two thirds consists largely of turgid polemic), which contains Marx's longest discussion of historical materialism—rich and exciting reading. There is a paperback edition of the relevant portion (C. J. Arthur, ed.) published by International Publishers in 1970.

With *The Communist Manifesto* and *The German Ideology* behind him, the reader can branch out in a number of directions. He should on no account miss Marx's analyses of current events in such brilliant pieces of polemical journalism as *The Eighteenth Brumaire of Louis Bonaparte* and *The Civil War in France* (both in the Moscow *Selected Works*). Marxian economics can be rather difficult, and a good introduction is provided either by *Wage-Labour and Capital,* written in 1848, or the 1865 *Value, Price and Profit* (also both contained in the Moscow *Selected Works*). The latter is a summary of the main ideas of *Capital* and, since it was a lecture delivered to British trade unionists of whose intellectual capacity Marx had a very low opinion, it is as simple as possible. *Capital,* Volume One, itself is by no means as difficult as is sometimes believed. The first 250 pages or so deal with rather abstract but perfectly intelligible economic concepts, but the second half contains analyses of Victorian capitalism which show not only Marx's historical method at work but also how great a literary talent he possessed. Volume Two is rather technical and only for the really keen; Volume Three, edited from the manuscripts, has none of the polish of Volume One but contains important material—particularly the last section on the Trinitarian formula.

For an appreciation of the genesis of *Capital* and its place in Marx's work as a whole, a reading of the *Grundrisse* is vital. It gives a fascinating picture of Marx at work. But it is also the most difficult of Marx's writings. For those who wish to tackle the entire 800 pages, there is a Penguin edition with an insightful introduction; for the less ambitious, Paladin has a much shorter selection with the most important passages.

No understanding of Marx is complete without some knowledge of the early writings. The most important are the *Economic and Philosophical Manuscripts* (translated in full in the Milligan and Bottomore editions). The particularly interesting sections are "Alienated Labor," "Private Property and Communism," and "Critique of Hegel's Dialectic," which should be read in that order and at least twice. (These three sections are also translated in the Easton and Guddat and McLellan editions.)

The best short edition of selected writings of Marx is that by Bottomore and Rubel, although the "classical" selection is that of the Moscow *Selected Works,* which has the advantage of mainly reproducing pieces whole, though there are no early writings and the commentary is sometimes rather tendentious. Most of the others suffer from being largely selections from the Moscow selections and do not include more recent new material. With this proviso, the two best are those edited by Tucker and by Bender. The forthcoming selection by McLellan is intended to be as widely representative as possible.

Now to the necessarily rather more subjective question of commentaries. There is the present writer's own *The Thought of Karl Marx: An Introduction.* Fischer's *Marx in His Own Words* and Sanderson's *The Political Ideas of Marx and Engels* are also good introductions. At a slightly more advanced level, two excellent commentaries are Avineri's *The Social and Political Thought of Karl Marx,* which emphasizes Marx's debt to Hegel, and Evans' *Marx,* which gives a good all-round analytical and historical introduction. A little more difficult is Ollman's *Alienation,* which offers a reinterpretation of Marx's thought in terms of that concept.

Turning to more specialized fields, two good books introducing Marx's sociology are Zeitlin's *Marxism: A Re-Examination* and Lefebvre's *The Sociology of Marx.* For Marx's politics, a book with a wealth of detail and accurate interpretation is Hunt's *The Political Ideas of Marx and Engels.* The best way to appreciate Marx's approach to history is to read some of its practitioners—Christopher Hill, Eric Hobsbawm, and Edward Thompson, for example—though a good account is to be found in Fleischer's *Marxism and History.* Marx's economics are definitely not easy, but probably the best introduction is Mandel's short *Introduction to Marxist Economic Theory,* followed by the same author's *The*

Formation of the Economic Thought of Karl Marx. Those who want something a bit more technical could try Desai's *Introduction to Marxian Economics.*

An area where a commentary of some sort is almost essential is Marx's early writings: the books by Dupré, Howard, and McLellan, all cover the ground with as much clarity and concision as possible. Kamenka's *The Ethical Foundations of Marxism* has a slightly more philosophical approach; Maguire's *Marx's Paris Writings* is the most extensive commentary available on the work of 1844; and Tucker's *Philosophy and Myth in Karl Marx* is a provocative and influential account of Marx as a pseudoreligious thinker.

Those interested in the orthodox Communist interpretation of Marx can read Garaudy's *Karl Marx: The Evolution of His Thought* or Lewis's *The Life and Teaching of Karl Marx.* The "classical" critique of Marx's historical materialism can be found in Acton, *The Illusion of an Epoch*, or Plamenatz, *German Marxism and Russian Communism.* As for biographies there are two excellent short ones by Berlin and by Blumenberg; Mehring had provided the standard full-length one for decades; and I hope that my own is comprehensive and reliable. This last also contains a fuller bibliography than space here permits.

MULTIVOLUME COLLECTIONS BY MARX

Works. New York: International Publishers, 1975ff. Written with Friedrich Engels.
The 1848 Revolutions, Surveys from Exile, The First International and After. D. Fernbach, ed. New York: Monthly Review, 1973–.
On Revolution, On Press Freedom and Censorship. S. Padover, ed. New York: McGraw-Hill, 1971–.

SINGLE-VOLUME COLLECTIONS BY MARX

Selected Works. Moscow, 1935. Written with Friedrich Engels.
Selected Writings in Sociology and Social Philosophy. T. B. Bottomore and M. Rubel, eds. London: Watts, 1956.

Reader. R. C. Tucker, ed. New York: Norton, 1971. Written with Friedrich Engels.

The Essential Writings. R. Bender, ed. New York: Harper & Row, 1972.

Selected Writings. D. McLellan, ed. New York: Oxford University Press, 1975.

Writings of the Young Marx on Philosophy and Society. L. D. Easton and K. H. Guddat, eds. New York: Doubleday & Co., 1967.

The Early Texts. D. McLellan, ed. New York: Barnes & Noble, 1971.

SINGLE WORKS BY MARX

The Communist Manifesto. A.J.P. Taylor, ed. New York: Penguin Books, 1967. Written with Friedrich Engels.

The German Ideology, Part One. C. Arthur, ed. New York: International Publishers, 1970. Written with Friedrich Engels.

The Grundrisse. M. Nicolaus, ed. New York: Monthly Review, 1973.

Capital. S. Moore and E. Aveling, trans. London, 1887.

Economic and Philosophical Manuscripts of 1844. D. J. Struick, ed. M. Milligan, trans. New York: International Publishing Co., 1971.

COMMENTARIES ABOUT MARX

Acton, H.B. *The Illusion of the Epoch*. New York: Routledge & Kegan, 1955.

Althusser, Louis. *For Marx*. B.R. Brewster, trans. New York: Pantheon, 1970.

Avineri, Shlomo. *The Social and Political Thought of Karl Marx*. New York: Cambridge University Press, 1971.

Berlin, Isaiah. *Karl Marx, His Life and Environment*. New York: Oxford University Press, 1939.

Blumenberg, Werner. *Portrait of Marx: An Illustrated Biography*. Douglas Scott, trans. New York: McGraw-Hill, 1972.

Dupré, Louis. *Philosophical Foundations of Marxism*. New York: Harcourt Brace Jovanovich, 1966.

Evans, Michael. *Marx*. New York: Barnes & Noble, 1975.

Fischer, Ernst. *Marx in His Own Words*. Anna Bostack, trans. New York: Herder & Herder, 1972.

Fleischer, Helmut. *Marxism and History*. London: Allen Lane, 1973.

Garaudy, Roger. *Karl Marx. The Evolution of His Thought*. New York: International Publishing Co., 1967.

Habermas, Jurgen. *Knowledge and Human Interests*. Jeremy J. Shapiro, trans. Boston: Beacon Press, 1971.

Howard, Dick. *The Development of the Marxian Dialectic*. Carbondale: Southern Illinois University Press, 1972.

Hunt, Richard. *The Political Ideas of Marx and Engels*. Pittsburgh: University of Pittsburgh Press, 1975.

Kamenka, Eugene. *The Ethical Foundations of Marxism*. New York: Routledge & Kegan, 1962.

Lefebvre, Henri. *Sociology of Marx*. Norbert Guterman, trans. New York: Pantheon, 1968.

Lewis, John. *The Life and Teaching of Karl Marx*. New York: International Publishing Co., 1965.

Lukács, Georg. *History and Class Consciousness*. Rodney Livingstone, trans. Cambridge: MIT Press, 1971.

McLellan, David. *Marx Before Marxism*. New York: Harper & Row, 1971.

——— *The Thought of Karl Marx: An Introduction*. New York: Harper & Row, 1972.

——— *Karl Marx: His Life and Thought*. New York: Harper & Row, 1974.

Mandel, Ernest. *Formation of the Economic Thought of Karl Marx*. Brian Pearce, trans. New York: Monthly Review Press, 1971.

——— *Introduction to Marxist Theory*. New York: Path Press, 1969.

Maguire, John. *Marx's Paris Writings: An Analysis*. New York: Barnes & Noble, 1973.

Marcuse, Herbert. *One Dimensional Man*. Boston: Beacon Press, 1964.

——— *Eros and Civilization*. Boston: Beacon Press, 1955.

Mehring, Franz. *Karl Marx*. Edward Fitzgerald, trans. New York: Humanities Press, 1936.

Ollmann, Bertell. *Alienation: Marx's Conception of Man in*

Capitalist Society. New York: Cambridge University Press, 1971.

Plamenatz, John. *German Marxism and Russian Communism.* New York: Longmans, Green, 1954.

Sanderson, J.B. *Interpretation of the Political Ideas of Marx and Engels.* New York: Fernhill, 1969.

Tucker, Robert C. *Philosophy and Myth in Karl Marx.* New York: Cambridge University Press, 1961.

Zeitlin, Irving M. *Marxism: A Re-Examination.* New York: Van Nostrand Reinhold Co., 1967.

INDEX

A selection of books published by Penguin
is listed on the following pages. For a complete list of books available from Penguin in
the United States, write to Dept. DG, Penguin Books, 299 Murray Hill Parkway, East
Rutherford, New Jersey 07073.

THE FREE AND THE UNFREE
A New History of the United States

Peter N. Carroll and David W. Noble

The Free and the Unfree is a "counterculture" survey of American history from pre-Columbian times to the post-Watergate era. Based largely on firsthand sources, the book focuses, in each period, on the dynamic relationship between the nation's ruling elite and its various "outgroups"—native Americans, blacks, women, ethnic minorities, and, most recently, young people. The book's bold conclusion is that these groups will be the saviors of the country's future—for they regard America as a "home" to care for, not as a "frontier" to be exploited.

THE OTHER AMERICA
Poverty in the United States

Michael Harrington

Here, with a new Introduction, is Michael Harrington's classic portrait of America's poor people. When it was first published, *The Other America* caused a sensation by exposing the seamy side of the Affluent Society. It is indeed a shocking report that covers the whole nation, from New York's Bowery through Arkansas's cotton fields to the lush fruit orchards of the West Coast. Unskilled workers, the aged, racial minorities— none of the groups that form the country's economic underworld is overlooked. But the book's greatest impact lies in its radical view of "the other America" as a self-perpetuating culture, a citadel of misery that only a massive and integrated program can overthrow.

ALL THE LIVELONG DAY
The Meaning and Demeaning of Routine Work

Barbara Garson

What do employees do all day in a tuna-fish cannery or a Ping-Pong plant? How do keypunchers, auto assemblers, and insurance clerks keep from going crazy? To find out, Barbara Garson traveled around the country for two years, spying out the games, the devices people use to restore meaning to jobs drained of meaning in the name of profit. She found resentment, humiliation, even sabotage; above all, she found that people "passionately want to work." "This is a loving book. It celebrates man's vitality and ingenuity under intense pressures designed to turn him into a machine"—*Christian Science Monitor*.

THE WORKING-CLASS MAJORITY

Andrew Levison

This outspoken book explodes myths about America's forgotten man, the blue-collar worker. Defining the working class as people "employed in essentially rote, manual labor," Andrew Levison shows that today's workers are not dwindling in number, are not financially secure, do not enjoy an easy middle-class way of life, and are, for the most part, neither racist nor conservative. The liberals who have despaired of the blue-collar man because of such misconceptions must face the facts. Only then will there emerge the "liberal-labor alliance" that Levison calls "our clearest hope for progress."

CHINESE SHADOWS
Simon Leys

Chinese Shadows takes us behind the shadowplay that
is all most Westerners ever see of today's China. Scath-
ingly critical of foreign journalists who whitewash the
Cultural Revolution, Simon Leys depicts the People's
Republic in shades both light and dark. Here are his
own experiences of living as a foreigner in Peking, of
taking the (heavily edited) grand tour through the great
cities and the Maoist shrines, of coping with the multi-
layered bureaucracy, and of meeting the admirable and
oppressed Chinese people. When *Chinese Shadows* appeared in France, it was hailed in *Le Monde* as "far and
away the best book of its kind—the most truthful, the
most sincere."

CHINA
The Quality of Life
Wilfred Burchett with Rewi Alley

For the past fifty years China has been in turmoil.
How have the Chinese people reacted to the enormous
changes, and where do they find themselves today?
In search of the answers to these questions, Rewi
Alley and Wilfred Burchett traveled the length and
breadth of China, talking to the people in villages and
communes, in their factories and farms. "Our central
interest," says Burchett, "has been to measure the
changes that have occurred in recent years in China
and to set them in perspective against what we knew
of old China. We tried to understand also how the ordi-
nary Chinese citizens conceive that much bandied-
about term: 'quality of life.' "